To Render Invisible

UNIVERSITY PRESS OF FLORIDA

Florida A&M University, Tallahassee
Florida Atlantic University, Boca Raton
Florida Gulf Coast University, Ft. Myers
Florida International University, Miami
Florida State University, Tallahassee
New College of Florida, Sarasota
University of Central Florida, Orlando
University of Florida, Gainesville
University of North Florida, Jacksonville
University of South Florida, Tampa
University of West Florida, Pensacola

University Press of Florida
Gainesville Tallahassee Tampa
Boca Raton Pensacola Orlando
Miami Jacksonville Ft. Myers Sarasota

TO RENDER
INVISIBLE

JIM CROW AND PUBLIC LIFE
IN NEW SOUTH JACKSONVILLE

ROBERT CASSANELLO

This book may be available in an electronic edition.

21 20 19 18 17 16   6 5 4 3 2 1

First cloth printing, 2013
First paperback printing, 2016

Library of Congress Cataloging-in-Publication Data
Cassanello, Robert.
To render invisible : Jim Crow and public life in New South Jacksonville /
Robert Cassanello.
p. cm.
Includes bibliographical references and index.
ISBN 978-0-8130-4419-4 (cloth: alk. paper)
ISBN 978-0-8130-6219-8 (pbk.)
1. African Americans—Florida—Jacksonville—History. 2. African Americans—
Civil rights—Florida—Jacksonville—History. 3. Racism—Florida—
Jacksonville—History. 4. Jacksonville
(Fla.) —Race relations. I. Title.
F319.J1C37 2013
323.1196'073075912—dc23
2012046692

University Press of Florida
15 Northwest 15th Street
Gainesville, FL 32611-2079
http://www.upf.com

Dedicated to Kenneth W. Goings,
who believed in me before I believed in myself

Contents

Figures

Tables

Acknowledgments

There have been many people who helped in various degrees toward the successful completion of this book. I would like to thank the staff at the Southern Historical Collection at the Wilson Library, University of North Carolina at Chapel Hill, as well as Special Collections at University of North Florida, and the P. K. Yonge Library of Florida History at the University of Florida. I was also greatly assisted by the staff at the National Archives and Records Administration, the Library of Congress, the Jacksonville Historical Society, Jacksonville Public Library, the State of Florida Archives, the Brevard Community College/University of Central Florida Joint-Use-Library, as well as the Interlibrary Loan department at the University of Central Florida Library. I have to make specific mention of the staff at these locations who went above and beyond to not only warmly greet me at each visit but who also searched far and wide for many documents and photos. For their continued professionalism and kindness, I would like to extend my gratitude to Boyd Murphree, David Nelson, James Cusick, Emily Lisska, Eileen Brady, Lauren Swain Mosley, Joanie Reynolds, and Andrew Todd.

I would like to make special notice of current and former students who helped locate research materials, found specific individuals in the U.S. Census Manuscripts, and created images in Adobe Photoshop for me. A portion of my royalties is probably owed to Heather Bollinger for the grunt work she performed without any complaint. Many thanks to Anne Ladyem McDivitt for her work on the images in this book. Kathy Parry entertained me with numerous conversations about race, space, and landscape; I learned so much from working with her.

I would like to thank the *Journal of Urban History* (SAGE/Society) for permission to republish part of an article in chapter 6 and the *Florida Historical Quarterly* for allowing me to republish part of an article in my conclusion.

I would also like to thank my colleagues at the University of Central Florida. Amelia Lyons for turning me on to Jürgen Habermas and *The Structural Transformation of the Public Sphere*. Connie Lester who made her office a safe refuge for me to talk about anything and everything I found on Jacksonville. My colleague and friend in the Department of Film, Lisa Mills, a Jacksonville native, who wanted to hear every detail about this research and who was always encouraged and excited by it. And to my former colleague, Lupe Garcia, who shared books and articles with me on the production of space in the city. And of course my old and new colleague Daniel S. Murphree who first challenged me in graduate school to not just say something but to say something transcendent about the history of Florida.

There have been many people over the years who provided important guidance and insight, and who, in some cases, mentored me and this project. W. Fitzhugh Brundage, David R. Roediger, Eric Arnesen, Raymond A. Mohl, and David R. Goldfield have given me encouragement over the years. Julian C. Chambliss and Alan Bliss deserve thanks because of our numerous conversations about my research and urban history. I must give special thanks to Paul Ortiz and Louis Kyriakoudes for reading the manuscript and providing the necessary comments that improved the quality of the revisions. I hope this work one day stands alongside their books, which provided the original inspiration for my research. Finally, I must shower much gratitude on Melanie Shell-Weiss who not only first pointed me to the literature on the production of space but always answered her phone or replied in e-mail when I needed encouragement and felt that the material was beyond my ability as a scholar.

I would also like to thank the fine staff at the University Press of Florida. This is my third book with them, and they have always been professional and never missed a deadline or failed to reply to any of my inquiries.

I want to personally thank Meredith Morris-Babb who believed in the project and shepherded the manuscript through its final channels.

I would like to thank my family, especially my mother who immediately shows my books off to all her friends moments after she receives her copy. My wife and also all of our four-legged children have made my life away from work exceptional during the last thirteen years. Because of them, I always look forward to coming home while away at work.

Finally there are no words in which I can express the debt I owe my former professor at Florida Atlantic University, Kenneth W. Goings. I have to disclose that the germ of this book really started when I was an undergraduate in his African American history course. It was a treat to sit in his class, where he would challenge us to think about the past in terms of the broad stories it presents rather than as names and dates to be memorized. Although the course content was on African American history, it was there I first learned the tools of the trade that provided success in my future pursuits. He would frequently tell us that to understand the lives of African Americans one had to know Ralph Ellison's *Invisible Man:* the novel became the decoder ring or template that made the material in class make sense. During so much of the class he returned to the theme of invisibility. After I graduated and spent my first years in front of college students, I did the best Ken Goings impersonation I could until I found my own voice. This book represents me finally achieving my own voice and bringing it full circle to where I can explain African American history through Ralph Ellison's *Invisible Man.* This is no impersonation; it is a testament to a wonderful teacher.

Introduction

The Color Line and the Public Sphere

W.E.B. Du Bois in the *Souls of Black Folk* concluded that "[t]he problem of the Twentieth Century is the problem of the color-line." This quote would frame our understanding of the black experience in America for most of the twentieth century. It is curious that both he and Frederick Douglass, who first coined the term in 1881, imagined the race problem in geographic terms as a line both concrete and abstract that separated whites and blacks in the South after the Civil War. For Douglass this line served a specific function in pushing African Americans into a racially subordinate position as a subaltern caste. Douglass too pointed to the political implications of these actions when he concluded that "wild apprehensions are expressed lest six millions of this inferior race will somehow or other manage to rule over thirty-five millions of the superior race." Decades later Du Bois asked the same question, "what are we going to tell the black voter in the South? Are we going to induce the best class of Negroes to take less and less interest in government, and to give up their right to take such an interest, without a protest?"[1]

What both Du Bois and Douglass were keenly aware of was the relationship the color line had to civic participation and public life. In the same way the color line is a story of geography, it is also a story of blacks and the public sphere. The color line and the history of blacks in the public sphere in the post–Civil War South share a parallel story. This too was not lost on C. Vann Woodward who first assumed that racial segregation was born out of social patterns or customs from slavery, but realized that its origins were actually long removed from slavery. Instead Woodward and later Edward Ayers would echo the fact that racial segregation was a modern artifact of the New South landscape. Howard N. Rabinowitz, however, was the first historian to really connect the emergence of the color line to black agency and black action in the South. Rabinowitz concluded that Southern whites imposed Jim Crow due to blacks being politically assertive and contentious in public life.[2]

Du Bois was one of the first scholars to embrace this sentiment. Reconstruction was a lost opportunity for blacks and white Southerners. Government agencies, such as the Freedmen's Bureau, and the resourcefulness of blacks in preparing for freedom through the building of schools, churches, and businesses fell victim to conservative white desires to push blacks out of the public sphere and into a state of second-class citizenship in the 1870s. To Du Bois the color line was not only a geographic construction of white supremacy, but also lived as a mental demarcation in the minds of African Americans—a phenomenon he referred to as the *veil*. The function of the color line for conservative whites in the South was not to remove blacks from public life in absolute terms, but to remove blacks from white public view that challenged Southern white perceptions of blacks as a race inherently inferior and socially unequal. Blacks who occupied subservient positions or who were outwardly deferential had a place within the white side of the color line. Blacks who were autonomous from white authority or who openly challenged white supremacy were considered a threat and thus were "out of place" within the white side of the color line.[3]

The physical and mental worlds of the color line existed as a cognitive dissonance to conservative white Southerners so that blacks who were "out of place" could be beyond view or invisible. The struggle for blacks to become visible to a majority population became a salient theme mined throughout the twentieth century by African American authors.

Celebrated writers such as Jean Toomer, Richard Wright, Nella Larsen, and Ralph Ellison fixated on the struggle for black men and women to be seen and heard as they truly were and not as whites perceived them through the filter of the color line. In some sense the racial tensions engendered during this period on both sides of the color line were precipitated by blacks making themselves "visible" to whites in public life.[4]

What we can conclude is that the history of the color line is as much a history of the geography of race relations as it is a history of blacks in the public sphere. The geography and the public sphere are interconnected since the discourse and debate that engenders a public sphere takes place in private and public spaces. As such, access and the production of space in those geographies can impact the discourse meant for the public sphere. The movement to push blacks into racially prescribed spaces had the added feature of limiting and sometimes silencing their voices in the public sphere. To understand this it is helpful to understand the public sphere and the production of space as concepts.

Jürgen Habermas conceived of the bourgeois public sphere as a way to explain the liberal democratic societies that emerged throughout Western Europe in the wake of the Enlightenment. Habermas believed that with the capitalist market economy the literate bourgeois class entered the public sphere to engage in political discourse and thus influence public policy. According to Habermas, the public sphere could be in the salons, bookshops, theatres, or the street, anywhere a discourse on the common good could take place and a political consensus could be formed. Previously these groups would be relegated to the private sphere of their homes and families or maybe even fraternal organizations. Throughout this time the public sphere expanded to include the bourgeois in a space that was democratized along with aristocrats or functionaries of the state. Habermas concluded that the bourgeois moved from the private sphere to the public sphere in this transition.[5]

In the 1990s, Habermas's public sphere was critiqued by feminist scholars. Joan B. Landes, Mary P. Ryan, and Nancy Fraser all pointed to the limits of the single public sphere and specifically where women fit into a unitary public sphere, especially when the public sphere was not democratized for them. Landes concluded that men masculinized the public sphere in order to push women out of it in Revolutionary France while Ryan concluded that nineteenth century white women activists pushed into the public sphere from the margins of antebellum society in the United States. Fraser synthesized these processes to conclude that there was not a single unitary public, but multiple publics, what she would describe as *subaltern counterpublics*. The emergence of these counterpublics was the result of societies being socially stratified and the groups and voices on the margins that did not have equal access to the democratized public sphere constructed public spheres on their own that could engage the bourgeois public sphere and push the subaltern discourse into the public sphere. The existence of these counterpublics demonstrated that the nature of public political discourse was inherently discursive when local communities were stratified or heterogeneous in nature. Fraser additionally expands on Habermas's notion of the theatre of the public sphere. Political discourse could be performed symbolically to critique the public sphere so that the greater public might be influenced by the discourse within one or more of the competing publics.[6]

Both Robert Asen and Daniel C. Brouwer conclude that the black public sphere represents the clearest indication of a counterpublic at work. According to them, the development of a black counterpublic helped to produce a collective group identity that evolved in opposition to the oppression from the dominant social group. Evelyn Brooks Higginbotham was one of the first historians to trace the development of a black public sphere through the black Baptist Church. The black church was a location where the black public sphere could engage outside the supervision of white authority. The black counterpublic served a dual function, according to Michael C. Dawson, who concludes that not only was its purpose to politically organize outside the dominant public sphere, but also for blacks to openly and publicly "reinsert themselves into the channels of public discourse."[7]

Historians for decades depicted a Jim Crow South not only as a nadir of race relations, but also absent of black political engagement and meaningful participation with the dominant public sphere. During the height of the civil rights movement, an entire generation of Revisionist historians assumed that blacks accommodating to racial segregation and disfranchisement was the only successful political strategy for a Southern population confronting lynchings, racial violence, and legal abandonment. Blair L. M. Kelley, in her study of the streetcar boycott movement, reminds us that as Jim Crow moved into the everyday lives of blacks,

African American activists organized and publicly confronted segregated public transportation. Political engagement in public spaces depended upon organizing and planning in private spaces. The public spaces of Jim Crow are iconic in the signs declaring "colored bathrooms" or "for whites only" that adorned public faculties and accommodations. Within black churches, schools, businesses, and fraternal organizations, however, blacks could meet in private to foster a consensus about the state of race relations, explore the meaning of black citizenship, and develop strategies to combat white supremacy. Thus racial segregation was not only a catalyst but also a loci for the black public sphere.[8]

The public sphere is dependent upon space, specifically public space. Henri Lefebvre argued that each society has shaped its space to fit its economic production and its political and social reproduction. Thus space is constructed, produced, and reproduced. According to Lefebvre, public space encodes and clothes social relations. Geographer David Harvey extends this discussion further to suggest that public spaces can be interpreted as the "geography of difference" where the construction of spaces, both public and private, is a discursive process between the state and groups on the margins. Thus public space can be a text to understand the process and nature of social stratification and the discourse between groups in the center and on the margins. Jessica Ellen Sewell, in her study of women and public space in San Francisco, points out that public space in the city is not only a "space for discourse" but also the theatre by which women moved from the private to the public sphere. According to Sewell public spaces were not democratized but gendered and segregated by sex and class.[9]

How a space is produced at times can depend upon discursive actions that take place in that space. Tim Cresswell, in his book *In Place/Out of Place* examines when and how spaces and places are reconstructed due to transgressions. Cresswell suggests that transgressions are acts of resistance in public places to reform a space by a group on the margin. These acts are usually symbolic in nature, but are interpreted by the center as "out of place" and cross some perceived social boundary. These transgressive acts typically create a response by state agents or actors for the majority group to exert control to "return order" to a place as it was perceived by the dominant center. Mike Davis, in his study of Los Angeles, makes the case that the police department was the institution that regulated public spaces and ordered them in a strict and "militarized" fashion. Over time Davis argued that public spaces become less public and less welcoming to the poor, homeless, and disfranchised residents of the city.[10] Since public space is the theatre in which the public sphere emerges, the state has a stake in producing public space. Thus if the public sphere becomes transgressive, discursive, and disorderly, then the state can reorder the public space and in turn quiet the discourse. In cases where the state is disinterested or restricted from reordering public spaces, private citizens then can also reorder space to respond to any perceived transgressions.

As Robin D. G. Kelley reminds us, transgressive actions were part of everyday interactions in the Jim Crow South. Sometimes these actions were overt and part of public life and other times these transgressive actions were connected to an underground network of "hidden transcripts." Paul Ortiz in his study of black political mobilization in Florida tracks the ways in which blacks organized in private spaces and interpersonal networks to politically engage with a conservative political culture bent on excluding them from the public sphere. As blacks were pushed to the margins, they pushed back in both open and covert ways.[11]

The South during the Reconstruction and New South eras gives us a window into understanding these processes in very stark ways. Coming on the heels of the Civil War, the social landscape of the South changed in very profound ways. African American slavery ended as a political, economic, and social system and thus the state tried to integrate blacks into Southern society absent of slavery as a system that defined social relations. This process brought with it a vibrant debate about the meaning of citizenship and its rights and responsibilities across racial and gender lines. Jacksonville, Florida, gives us a location where these economic, political, and social transformations are writ large. Before the Civil War Jacksonville was a small port city that the U.S. Army found useful in capturing and defending. The city then became a nexus for freedmen and women as well as Northern missionaries and merchants who all envisioned the city's future along the lines of demographic, economic, and industrial expansion. Because of this rapid growth, social relations remained in flux.

In regard to the public sphere, the end of the Civil War brought people, groups, and institutions into the public for the first time. The most obvious of these were African Americans. Although no space is absolutely democratized, Reconstruction in Jacksonville represented a time when public space was the most democratized. The presence of federal troops and the integration of black men and sympathetic Northern white Republicans into the public sphere helped to directly move blacks out of the private sphere and into the public. Indirectly poor and working-class whites too entered the public sphere during the same time, followed by women both black and white. As the era of Reconstruction ended, the New South period epitomized a point when social stratification became more contested, and thus the public space in the city was not only a theatre but also a battleground where the social and political discourse could evolve from disorderly to violent over time. State and municipal governments used the pretext of "restoring order" during this time as a tool to limit public speech. Lisa Keller, in her book *Triumph of Order*, demonstrates that these issues were not limited to only the United States. She compared New York with London to show how both governments throughout the nineteenth century reconstructed public space in response to potential violence or actual violence and the resulting impact this process had on public speech.[12]

Additionally Keller's thesis reflects a growing trend in social science literature known as "right to the city" or the "end of public space." In works by Marcelo Lopes de Souza, Margit Mayer, and James Holston, these authors conclude that subaltern populations in the Global South are pushed out of the city centers where there are public spaces for speech. These subaltern populations remain outside the city where these residents are left voiceless in this geographic shift. As such these populations on the margins create an independent public sphere that challenge the dominant public sphere. Although these studies are contemporary and geographically dispersed, at their kernel is the process of social stratification and marginalization of a subaltern population.[13] While this examination fits the Global South, it also provides a window to understand the racialization of space and the public sphere in the urban South after the Civil War.

When Woodward researched and wrote *The Strange Career of Jim Crow* he was situated in a time and place that was challenging legal segregation and its meaning. Today scholars are situated in a world that is increasingly interconnected. So much so that for over a decade historians of the South and the nation are demanding that we challenge ourselves to move beyond narrative models that promote a place or region as exceptional.[14] I challenge the reader to think about the process of racialization that pushed blacks to the margins of Southern society and consider those systems in more universal terms that would translate to subaltern populations across time and space. The story of the color line and the public sphere would ring familiar to women during the French Revolution as described by Joan B. Landes, Cold War Gay and Lesbians as examined by Michael Warner as well as the subaltern populations in the Global South.

1

Re-Ordered Spaces

Jürgen Habermas conceived of the bourgeois public sphere as a "space for democracy" that was predicated on unity and equality. This was important because in order for a discourse on the common good to emerge, citizens of unequal social and economic backgrounds needed a democratic space where a political consensus could be formed. Although critics have pointed out that unity or even equality in the public sphere was not indispensable to the formation of a public, competing groups with varied interests depended upon democratized spaces to formulate opinion and usher a discursive debate into the public sphere.[1] Space as organized in a slave society in the South was not democratized for black political engagement or participation even for free blacks. The Civil War created a new set of circumstances for the production of space in the South because the military presence existed above local and state government and operated as the state for the rest of the 1860s. In addition to the military, many white Northern missionaries came to the city and represented an influx of a new bourgeois public whose social outlook conflicted with the native-born white bourgeois. The ways in which spaces, both public and private, were ordered before the war no longer had relevance as the war came to the streets of Jacksonville.

As the Civil War abolished the institution of slavery, it also recast space within the city as new—really yet to be defined. Legislation, custom, and practice all helped to create spaces in antebellum Jacksonville as a reflection of the social system of slavery. Unlike before the war, Northern whites, blacks, and the federal government would have some role in the construction of new and redefined spaces. For blacks and Northern whites the reconstruction of public space held out an opportunity to redress the social ills born out of a slave society. The spirit of constitutional equality that would embody the Fourteenth Amendment and various civil rights legislation would be the template by which blacks and many Northern whites reconceived public and private spaces. For blacks and Northern missionaries, equal access to public spaces would clothe blacks in freedom, equality, and most important citizenship.

Stephanie M. H. Camp concluded that geography transmitted not only a social reality but also a discourse on plantation life. Antebellum planters promoted a spatial geography that kept their bonded populations, in addition to free blacks, nearby as a means to affirm white authority over black life and to discourage truancy, escape, as well as insurrection. Conversely, she pointed out that bonded men and women engaged in the geography of freedom and resistance that kept distance between them and the fixtures of white antebellum authority.[2] The Civil War would be the catalyst that put this spatial geography in flux. As federal troops controlled northeast Florida by 1864 and 1865, the spatial patterns of slavery soon gave way to the geography of freedom and later racial equality. In the closing weeks of the war, Jacksonville's *Florida Union* reported that in the plantation belt, "negroes who had been well treated by their former masters were not only willing, but eager to remain with them," as a way to suggest familiar patterns of cultural geography would persist in postwar Florida.[3] Ester Hill Hawks, a teacher and Northerner abolitionist who came to Jacksonville in 1864 to open a school for freedmen and women, noticed that the city became a magnet for former slaves recently escaped and freed from places as far as Tallahassee and even South Carolina.[4] As was the case with the Underground Railroad, for many former slaves the geography of freedom translated into a distance between them and the plantations they previously worked and white authority itself.

Figure 1. Freed slaves gather in front of the Provost Marshall's headquarters, Jacksonville, 1864. Jacksonville Historical Society Photographic Collection.

Black individual and collective actions as a discourse on freedom were not unusual in the South. Eric Foner uncovered numerous black actions ranging from moving distances near and far or building churches and schools as tests of freedom so former slaves could know they were truly freed and autonomous from white control. Without slavery as the legal mechanism that defined social status, the proximity of blacks to whites would be not only another test of freedom but also evidence that private and public spaces were democratic and did not embed blacks with second-class status. According to one resident of Jacksonville, Calvin L. Robinson, he claimed that before the war local blacks and whites were racially segregated within the same church where blacks sat in the back or in balconies. He further commented that for larger denominations blacks built their own buildings for the local pastor to visit after preaching at the white church. In a letter to *Zion's Herald and Wesleyan Journal*, Robinson told of the Civil War creating a "different state of things," where blacks and whites sat integrated in the same churches. The democratized spaces were not universally welcomed and Robinson cautioned that "grave difficulties

Table 1. Church denominations in Duval County, 1860–1870

	Roman Catholic	Presbyterian	Methodist	Baptist	Episcopal	Seventh Day Adventist	Total
1860	1	1	2	2	1	0	7
1870	1	1	7	5	2	1	17

Source: Historical Census Browser. Retrieved 26 October 2011 from the University of Virginia, Geospatial and Statistical Data Center, http://www.fisher.lib.virginia.edu/collections/stats/histcensus/index.html.

[would] arise" from these new practices because of how "deeply the notion of caste fix[ed] themselves in the heart of man."[5]

Even Northern white missionaries who came to the city during this time opened schools absent of fixed racial policies. Teachers from the North expected to and in some cases taught the children of local blacks and whites in the same classroom. Albeit there were no policies or legal restrictions on space in the classroom, many local whites refused to allow their children to learn alongside blacks.[6] In Jacksonville's wartime urban milieu many former slaves and other African Americans practiced the geography of freedom not as one of distance from whites but as one of proximity to them in the private spaces of schools and churches as a way to test and acknowledge their own freedom.

Freed bondsmen and women were not the only blacks who tested and questioned their newfound freedom. A number of African American soldiers, many of whom lived in the North, came with the Union Army and a hope that the South would be fertile ground to test the federal government's commitment to equal rights in a country that recently banished chattel slavery. For the African Americans in the Union Army, they hoped that Jacksonville could be transformed as a Southern place where public and private spaces could be equally shared between them and whites. One soldier writing to a Philadelphia newspaper in December 1864 expressed his hope that "Johnny will make his appearance; we want to introduce him to some of Uncle Sam's Anti-Billions Pills."[7] Soldiers often referred to bullets as "pills" and anti-billions pills were herbal medications taken in the nineteenth century as a precaution to avoid future sickness. For the U.S. Colored Troops (U.S.C.T.) they believed that slavery, racism, and inequality were the sicknesses inhabiting the South in which the Union effort was meant to cure. Richard M. Smith, the drummer for Company A, 3rd Division, noted that

The bonds of slavery are shivering to pieces before the conquering arm of Almighty power, and the prejudice against color and race is disappearing before liberty and justice, as the mist flees from before the morning sun. The black man has proven himself a patriot, a hero, and a man of courage. He is preparing by education, to be a true and worthy citizen of the United States.[8]

Smith was not the only black soldier who recognized the connection between citizenship and equality at stake in the outcome of the war.

The notion of rights and the belief that rights are engendered equally was first communicated in letters sent to black Northern newspapers like Philadelphia's *Christian Recorder*. Many soldiers stationed in Jacksonville complained and protested their treatment by the federal government who did not pay them as regularly as white troops and who many believed promoted unqualified white soldiers over more qualified black soldiers.[9] One sergeant with the Massachusetts Company H, 54th Division, pointed out:

Let the black man rise on some high stage, and civilians promoted and put over colored soldiers, when they do not know how to draw a sword yet; for they have never had any military education before they came to our regiment to learn, and the colored men that know must be under such men before they can be promoted to lieuten- ant. . . . Let us hear from Congress very soon, and let them pay us our rights. . . . the army will prosper and be victorious in every battle that shall be fought, and not until they recognize the rights of the sable-skinned warrior.[10]

In the last year of the war, black troops promoted a discourse on the meaning of freedom that questioned the federal government's commit- ment to racial equality.

Although public and private spaces were more democratic as a result of the war, the concept of democratized space was not absolute and of- ten inconsistently enforced by the military. The irony of how space was transformed was not lost on Sergeant Major Rufus Sibb Jones with the 8th U.S.C.T. He remarked that "[i]t must be humiliating to those who once lived in style, and owned slaves, to see their property, and that of others, occupied as hospitals by negro soldiers from the North. It often happens here, that the mistress and servant eat together in sutler stores."[11]

Although Jones witnessed examples of public and private spaces in the city constructed through more democratic means, he also noted that these spaces were juxtaposed with scenes of former Confederates and their sympathizers welcomed by the military order to open shops and businesses when Northern blacks were denied the same requests. Jones lamented these social contradictions in his letter back home; however, he held out some hope because one white denizen of the encampment, an "old white dog" named "Lion" had "no objection to being among black soldiers."[12]

Black soldiers were not the only group of people wrestling with the newfound boundaries of public space: the white commanders of the Union forces often concerned themselves with the meaning of public and private interactions between white officers and blacks. Since space encoded social distinctions, the military was leery of the actions of their white officers being misinterpreted as an institutional commitment to social equality. Two white officers traveling aboard the steamship *Mary Benton* in the summer of 1864 were punished by the military for "Conduct Unbecoming an Officer and Gentleman." In both cases the officers were reported to be indiscreet and too familiar with black women who were traveling onboard the ship. Both officers were overheard to have made explicit sexual advances to these women, which were witnessed by other officers and black soldiers under their command. In another case in the summer of 1865, Captain Henry M. Jordan with U.S.C.T. Company I, 34th Division, was punished for drinking with his soldiers in his quarters and was reported to have been seen dancing and wrapped in an embrace while lying in bed with a black woman in full view of black soldiers under his command. According to the court-martial transcripts of these three cases the judges were just as concerned to learn not only what happened but also if the black soldiers who witnessed this behavior were under the impression these actions reinforced notions of social equality.[13] For the judges acting on behalf of the Union Army, actions in public and private spaces could transmit social meanings these military officials wanted desperately to avoid.

Although the military tried to punish white officers for leaving blacks with the possible impression of social equality, their official efforts left blacks with very mixed signals. Second Lieutenant Henry K. Cady of U.S.C.T. Company D, 34th Division, was punished for a series of racially charged comments made publicly and privately to other white soldiers.

Witnesses claimed he stated that "the dammed nigger did not belong to the human race that the form of his head showed it." Additionally Cady described a trip to Africa where he claimed to have witnessed "Negroes hanging from trees with their tails and eating bananas and that slave catchers cut their tails off and seared them with a hot iron." Finally, according to the testimony against Cady, witnesses claimed that Cady would often profess that he "did not want any dammed Nigger as an equal with him." All of the racially charged accusations Cady confessed to uttering under oath—all of which he claimed did not violate military policies and were within his rights of free speech.[14]

The punishment of black soldiers by the military authority demonstrated the ways in which actions in public spaces were part of a larger discourse on racial equality and the democracy of space. In the last years of the Civil War, the U.S. Army was charged with preserving law and order in the city for most of the 1860s. A large number of African Americans remained during and after the War—soldiers and civilians alike. The most high profile case of black resistance to military authority occurred in October 1865 in what was known as the Jacksonville Mutiny.

Although the Jacksonville Mutiny has the distinction of being the last time U.S. soldiers were executed for mutiny, it represented only one point in a long chain of episodes where black soldiers publicly questioned their treatment at the hands of military authority.[15] Since the spring of 1864, African American soldiers were punished by the army in very public ways. When a black soldier committed an infraction, white officers publicly humiliated him by tying him up by his thumbs with his feet barely touching the ground. Public punishments were not unusual for the military; however, many commanders stopped because this practice was too reminiscent of actions planters took to punish slaves. In Jacksonville, white commanders continued this practice unimpeded.[16]

Resistance to this punishment was not uncommon for black soldiers. Many times the punishment was not carried out due to this resistance. In May 1864 Charles A. Merritt was accused of being absent without leave when he refused to go on guard duty. When Second Lieutenant B. F. Buckley found Merritt reading, he confronted him. Buckley claimed that Merritt responded by laughing in an "insolent way." Buckley ordered Merritt strung up for disobeying orders after which Merritt pulled a hatchet from under his shirt and said he would "attack anyone who tried to put him under confinement." Commanding officer Captain Sherman Conant instead put him in a sweatbox for a few days. In a similar incident in June 1864, Sergeant Stephen G. Chew ordered John Q. Adams on police duty to which Adams pulled out a pocketknife and refused. Chew ordered him tied up and Adams exclaimed, "you won't unless you kill me first." Chew backed down and pressed charges against him instead. In September 1864 during another altercation, this time Sergeant Patrick Cannaavn ordered Thomas Wright to unload forage while Wright engaged in a very public resistance to military authority. Cannaavn brought out rope to tie Wright up as punishment. Wright called him a "cowardly son of a bitch" and threatened to get his "revolver and shoot him" if he tried to tie him up.[17]

Not all soldiers were successful in avoiding this public punishment. Charles Sewell was tied up for refusing to come to inspection in August 1864. In addition to being tied up, he was further humiliated by being gagged after requesting food and water. The sense of unfairness and injustice in these public punishments were not lost only on the black soldiers. In March 1864 three black soldiers were hanged for the crime of "violating the person of a white woman." According to reports their bodies were displayed for "twenty four hours as a lesson to others." Esther Hill Hawks, a white Northern missionary, noticed that local black soldiers sobbed at the execution. She wrote that General Truman Seymour turned to the black soldiers in the audience and said, "Served them right, now let any other man try it if he dares." To which Hawks observed that "If the same measure had been meted out to white officers and men who have been guilty of the same offense towards black women, Gen. S. might have grown hoarse in repeating his remarks." Hawks was sanguine in noting that the execution "spread a feeling of gloom over our camp." Throughout 1864 black soldiers were cognizant of the ways in which their behavior was treated differently than their white counterparts.[18] Individually these actions may seem merely as disobedience of military authority; however, these cases cumulated into a debate concerning public punishment and the humiliation of black soldiers.

Two incidents in September 1865 laid the groundwork for the October mutiny. Sergeant Jack Middleton ordered Samuel Johnson tied up for urinating around his quarters. Johnson pulled out his bayonet and threatened anyone who tried to tie him up. Later when Second Lieutenant Henry K. Cady ordered a black solider tied up, sympathetic men freed him at least three times, which infuriated Cady who ordered guards to make sure it did not continue to happen.[19] According to U.S. Army

General Court-Martial records, throughout most of 1865 black soldiers either did not resist this punishment or were not punished in this way as there were no court-martials denoting this behavior. These September events along with the incidents of public punishments over the course of the previous year set the stage for the mutiny.

On October 29th, a black soldier was arrested allegedly for stealing molasses from the camp kitchen. After some resistance, Lieutenant Colonel John L. Brower, regiment commander, ordered the man strung up by his thumbs. Jacob Plowden, a soldier previously court-martialed for disobeying orders, objected to the public punishment and to the treatment of the fellow soldier. Plowden claimed that this humiliating punishment was only recently introduced to the regiment and charged that white soldiers were not punished the same way. Captain George Walrath testified that Plowden repeated this refrain over and over again. Plowden was reported to have stirred up sympathy with soldiers nearby who formed a crowd and advanced on their comrade still hanging by his thumbs. By this time Joseph Nathaniel was said to be leading the crowd of upwards of twenty men as Brower fired into the mob wounding one soldier. Lieutenant George Greybill and Walrath claimed everyone except Plowden ran to their tents and retrieved their weapons. Richard Lee said "Come on boys" and led the crowd back to free the punished soldier. Black noncommissioned officers tried to remove weapons from as many of the men as possible to quell the riot. In the disturbance Brower was shot in the thumb and hauled off to the kitchen for safety. Eventually white officers and black noncommissioned officers restored order and eleven men were rounded up, arrested, and court-martialed. The army eventually concluded that six of them were the ringleaders, and those men were summarily executed on 1 December 1865 at Fort Clinch in Fernandina.[20]

The Jacksonville Mutiny should not be taken as a discrete incident but part of a longer discourse between black soldiers and white military authority concerning displays of punishment in public places and egalitarian methods of adjudicating behavior between whites and blacks. Although the mob that formed might have seemed spontaneous to the single event in October 1865, the mob was the fruition of grievances against the military acting as the state. These actions by military commanders reminded blacks that public spaces were not democratized, so these militant actions engendered a debate concerning how space could be produced for public punishment.

African Americans in Jacksonville were not the only group of people who held out hope that the social practices of the past would give way to new patterns of social organizing based on more democratic principles. Northern missionaries came to Jacksonville in large numbers in the last year of the war committed to a transformation of the social environment armed only with biblical parables. One such woman named Emma B. Eveleth epitomized this philosophy when she recounted a story of a poor white women she tried to convince to attend her school alongside black pupils. She recalled not having seen any blacks in the area in worse shape than this woman and concluded:

> I could not help thinking it is not the color of their skin, that makes any one degraded, but their habits. If people are crushed down all their lives by the heel of oppression, can we expect them to rise all of a sudden & be a bright intelligent class of community, without even the dust of their past conditions clinging to them. . . . There is a hope that when slavery is really dead, & the spirit of caste is banished, they may arise & be equal to the colored people.[21]

Eveleth saw no social distinction between poor whites and blacks that could not be explained through environment or socioeconomic policies. In fact in her estimation, many blacks appeared socially superior to the poorest whites.

Timothy Willard Lewis, a Methodist minister from Massachusetts, came to Jacksonville in the spring of 1864 to assist the wounded after the Battle of Olustee. He described the following scene upon his arrival:

> Without distinction of nation, religion, or color, they were kindly assisted by their comrades and civilians. Prejudice and cast [sic] were forgotten in this hour of calamity. I saw a brave colored soldier, with one leg shattered, tenderly borne between two white men, with both arms around their necks. The question of complexion was not thought of then. Common dangers and sufferings inspire a common humanity.[22]

While Eveleth hoped to proselytize egalitarian spaces in the classroom, Lewis projected the Union Army would emerge as the institution by which the social order of the South could be transformed. In a letter to a Northern newspaper, Lewis sanguinely prayed, "Lord speak to the spiritual Gideons in our Israel, that they may lead the select host into the department of the South to battle successfully for God and Liberty. If this be done, a glorious future is before us as a nation, but if neglected all is lost."[23]

For many of the Northern missionaries, education and upbringing seemed to be the cause of social inequality. Calvin L. Robinson had come to Jacksonville from Boston only four years before the war. Like the Northern missionaries, liberal Christian thought and theology informed Robinson and helped to construct his view of Southern society. Similar to Eveleth and Lewis, Robinson believed the difference between blacks and whites in the South was one of experience and training, not a difference defined by inherent characteristics of their so-called civilizations. Unlike black troops who associated their equal rights as citizens with the war effort, many white Northerners instead associated equal rights as part of a universal Christian fellowship. Since Robinson had lived in Jacksonville before the war and was a member of the evangelical community in the North, he tried to make sense out of the problems facing Northerners during the reconstruction. Robinson explained that the reason why Southerners had lost the egalitarian message in their Christian worship was due to church members often being less "zealous" coupled with "exemplary Christians" populating congregations in fewer numbers compared to the North. As echoed in the observations of Eveleth and Lewis, Robinson too believed that social distinctions in the city were related to "the peculiar influences and training, under which Southern people come up and from the sad defects of character engendered by that training."[24]

The schools that Northern white missionaries established seemed to be the place where these experiments of democratized space would be employed. Although the classrooms were private spaces, they did demonstrate the limits of democratically produced space in the South and showed how the discourse of the meaning of racial equality in the public sphere entered these private spaces. By 1865, Northern missionaries and the Freedman's Bureau established schools to teach the recently freed bondsmen and women as well as their children. Northern missionaries wanted desperately to reach out to poor whites and opened schools for the co-education of the races.[25] The Cookman Institute was probably the most well-known school educating African Americans in the city. The school was founded in 1873 by members of the Trinity Church with Samuel B. Darnell serving as pastor and principal during its first decades. The school was originally conceived around preparing students for "manual

Table 2. School attendance in Duval County, 1870

Total	White Male	White Female	Black Male	Black Female
1,598	312	294	485	507

Source: Historical Census Browser. Retrieved 4 March 2012 from the University of Virginia Geospatial and Statistical Data Center, http://www.fisher.lib.virginia.edu/collections/stats/histcensus/index.html.

labor" or industrial education but soon promoted a curriculum of liberal arts education as well as some seminary preparation for black clergy.[26] By this time there were no public high schools—either black or white—so Darnell and the other founders hoped that Cookman would serve to prepare future black civic and spiritual leaders under white guidance and supervision until blacks could sustain such institutions on their own.

Also during this time, the Freedman's Aid Society took over the Stanton Normal School, which originally opened as a public school for blacks after the war but passed between public and private hands throughout this time. Stanton and Cookman took in white students, but very few. Stanton in the late 1860s recorded only one white pupil who was assigned a teacher reserved for the white students that more than likely was a compromise to outside pressure. Cookman enrolled only Darnell's daughter during the late 1880s. Both Stanton and Cookman were integrated spaces with strictly drawn hierarchical spheres defined by race. Day-to-day operations, management, and instruction were left to whites, although some blacks did teach. Students, however, were almost exclusively African American.[27] Although many white Northerners conceived of these schools as integrated spaces, there was a consensus among them that Northern educated white Christians would oversee and control that space, since to them, Southern blacks were not ready to teach and preach equally alongside whites.

Some African Americans in the city were not completely satisfied with the black public and private schools. In 1876 John R. Scott, a pastor with the African Methodist Episcopal (AME) Church organized an effort to open a school to train African American teachers. Since Cookman and Stanton were both geared to that same mission, Scott's effort was an attempt to create a school where black instructors and administrators oversaw the curriculum and operations of the school and thusly would oversee those spaces autonomous from white control. This was probably not a challenge to Darnell or other whites who taught in black schools since their efforts were universally praised by local blacks. If this effort was successful its fruit did not spring forth in Jacksonville, because after Scott died a group of pastors in the AME Church sought to open an industrial arts school modeled on the Hampton Institute in memory of Scott's earlier attempt.[28]

Schools were not the only private spaces that transmitted a meaning about social equality. Along with churches and schools the home too became a democratized space. Jesse Brooks, an escaped slave and Union soldier, reportedly abandoned his family to marry his former mistress in December 1865. The Union chaplain refused to marry them due to the fact that his bride was white, which caused an outrage with many of the Northern missionaries who tried to talk the chaplain out of his "foolishness." By February 1866 the *Jacksonville Times* disparagingly recorded seven white women living with black men throughout the city. The *Daily Florida Union* even reported a story from Madison County where local white vigilantes broke into the home of a white man and whipped him for marrying a black woman. When the widow of a white Jacksonville merchant married a black man in 1876, the newspaper reported that white and black residents gathered around the judge's office to voice their protest to the union.[29] The home and the family had always been a private space, but with the end of the war it too entered into a discourse on the nature of race and racial policy in the South.

In August 1865, the *Jacksonville Herald* reprinted an editorial from the former Union general and Ohio gubernatorial candidate Jacob Dolson Cox regarding racial policies in the South. In it, Cox promoted a "separation of the races" because he believed that Southern whites would eventually return to civic society and electoral power and soon take out their hostility and vengeance over the war on the black race. He argued that a complete and strict separation from Southern whites would assist the black "race" as a civilization so that "[c]olored men of talent and intelligence would not make a vain struggle for the empty name of being lawyers without briefs, merchants without trade [and have the opportunity] to take rank according to their character and ability."[30] Cox imagined a reservation of land in the South exclusively occupied by people of African descent that would grow separate and parallel to a white South. Although Cox's views were repudiated by liberal Northern newspapers of the time, the germ at the center of his proposal would have some salience to the next generation of Southern blacks and whites.[31] Cox, along with many native white residents, believed that integrated spaces were merely an experiment doomed to failure.

These issues were coming to the fore when in August 1865, President Andrew Johnson's provisional governor, William Marvin, gave a speech in Jacksonville promoting the forthcoming Constitutional Convention and declared that the new Constitution would "recognize the new order of things, and secure freedom to all alike." This was part of a statewide tour to assuage any tensions held over from the war. In these speeches Marvin mapped out his vision for the postslavery government of Florida and his philosophical underpinnings of equal rights under the law.[32] On a stop in Quincy, Florida, two months later, Marvin stated:

> As citizens, before the law, the freedmen must be in all respects our equals. I do not mean that as a race they are, or can be made, during many generations, if ever, the equals personally of the Caucasian race, or can enjoy the same political or social positions; but that is no reason why Constitution or law should discriminate against them.[33]

Even though Marvin was born in New York and was a Unionist during the war, he spent much of his adult life in Florida and served as a politician and judge dating back to the state's territorial years. Marvin and other white Florida native residents differed from Northern missionaries in their belief that black progress would become apparent only after generations of uplift under white supervision and control. Additionally Marvin concluded that blacks as a "race" of people were inherently below all whites no matter their class or educational background. These attitudes were embedded by law in the first legislative session of the new state government when it prescribed the strict separation of the races in all public space. According to the law the punishment for violating this order was to "stand in the pillory for one hour, or be whipped, not exceeding thirty-nine stripes, or both."[34]

With the 1865 State Constitution, blacks did not hold out much hope that democratically produced spaces would engender a sense of racial equality with whites. However, spaces were no longer inherently or legally proscribed loci of black subordination and white control. Instead, spaces—both public and private—were a middle ground where the meaning of space and racial equality could be negotiated as part of a broader discourse of the place where blacks fit into the public sphere.

2

Democratized Space

The Civil War ushered in a process by which public and private spaces within Jacksonville were in a state of flux. Although not absolute "spaces of democracy," blacks did enjoy greater freedom from white authority and used the production of space as a way to question the meaning of freedom. The military occupied Jacksonville from the end of the Civil War until the end of the 1860s. As such, the federal government through military agents and agencies operated if not as the state at least at times as an arbitrator over state and municipal government on behalf of blacks.

The military often mediated between blacks and local native whites unwilling to adjust to the new social ordering born out of the end of slavery. Since spaces were in a state of transition, blacks mobilized in the public spaces to engage all levels of government: federal, state, and municipal alike. Democratized space and entrance into the public sphere were tied together for black activists who voiced in both the private and public spaces their political ambitions to define and preserve their rights as citizens. As the Civil War ended, many blacks took to the public spaces in an effort to assert themselves in the public sphere for the first time. Blacks questioned their place as residents of a postslavery South and specifically whether the end of slavery was the equivalent of citizenship.

Blacks in Jacksonville, however, did not wait until the Fourteenth Amendment to demand rights as citizens, the most sacred of which was the franchise. Local whites in the newspapers engaged in a vigorous debate concerning the extent and contours of the black franchise. A July 1865 edition of the *Florida Union* reprinted a *New York Herald* editorial torpedoing universal black male suffrage and instead suggested only blacks who served in the military, owned real estate, were literate, or those who were in good standing with their church at least five years before the war deserved the right to vote. The reprinting of this editorial was to suggest that even in the North universal black male suffrage was not a foregone conclusion. This was not a consensus opinion in the city. A few months later the *Jacksonville Herald* claimed that throughout the state even "the most violent secessionists" favored universal male suffrage. This statement caused both the *Florida Union* and *Floridian and Journal* to rebuke such "reports."[1] The *Jacksonville Herald* during this time frequently questioned the meaning of black citizenship and its relationship to the franchise. The *Florida Union* went so far as to refer to the associate editor of the *Herald* as the "fuglemen" for social equality and miscegenation because of such support. *Herald* editors called the peculiar conditions by which black men could not vote the consequence of "southern citizenship." The *Herald* summed up their feelings by stating, "If all political rights are to be withheld from our new made freedmen, let them go down but as they sink stripped of everything but the privilege of breathing God's air, don't disgrace the name of citizen by applying it to such things."[2]

The *Florida Union* accused the *Jacksonville Herald* of organizing black troops in the fall of 1865 and encouraging them to demand the right to vote as a reward for their loyal wartime service. These meetings were held to protest the 1865 Constitutional Convention, which met in Tallahassee in late October. Delegates, along with Governor William Marvin, crafted a constitution that limited the franchise to white men over the age of twenty-one, and not only disfranchised black men but also anyone serving in the military stationed throughout the state. Opponents of black male suffrage speculated that black men who were still receiving pay from the federal government and loyal to Republican organs like the *Jacksonville Herald* would be easily organized as a voting bloc and blindly vote

the ways of their "patrons." The *Florida Times* expressed a similar sentiment questioning whether a race held in bondage could "intelligently"
practice the franchise. The editor of the *Florida Times,* however, argued
that "sound policy requires that the freedmen of the south should not be
admitted immediately to the right of suffrage," until a "system of *universal education*" would make "universal suffrage . . . safe and politic."[3] As
spaces throughout the city were in a state of flux, so was the legal status
of blacks. Whites held a variety of opinions concerning the meaning and
parameters of black citizenship.

Black men in Jacksonville did not sit idly by as the local press, constitutional delegates, and the governor debated the contours of black citizenship and its privileges. In September 1865 black soldiers and "citizens"
held public meetings at the Baptist Church. Although the church was a
private space, it became the loci to organize the political discourse that
would emerge in the public sphere during this time. Since blacks could
create and oversee these private spaces autonomous from white control or
supervision, it became an ideal place to mobilize a consensus to push the
idea of universal black male citizenship within the public sphere. Alonzo
Williams, Lewis Wright, and Bird Miller were appointed to prepare resolutions to petition the Constitutional Convention. Blacks attending the
meetings thanked Governor Marvin for advocating the rights of freedom
without regard to color or race, yet argued that in order for blacks to
protect their rights as freedmen, they "should be allowed a voice in the
selection of those who are to frame our laws" as well as "a uniform system
of suffrage." Leaders at the meeting then planned to move the consensus
that emerged from the private space into the public sphere by traveling
the petition throughout the state for signatures and finally delivering it
to state political leaders, constitutional delegates, and top officers in the
Freedmen's Bureau in Tallahassee.[4]

Although the Constitutional Convention and governor did not recognize black male suffrage as a condition of citizenship, they did abolish
slavery and provide for some nominal protections for blacks under the
1865 Florida Constitution. Locally however, the Jacksonville mayor and
alderman issued a number of ordinances in January 1866 repealing local
slave codes that provided the rights for blacks to freely travel, assemble,
organize, and celebrate throughout public and private spaces. The new
ordinances abolished any legal definitions and policies directed solely toward "slaves," "Free Negroes," and "Mulattoes." The new ordinances also

abolished legal white authority over blacks in public and private spaces. Included in this was rescinding the requirement that "Free Negroes" and "Mulattoes" be assigned a white guardian as well as the prohibition of "whipping slaves and free persons of color in the Public Market."[5]

All these efforts did not in fact create democratized spaces for everyone. Also repealed, as part of this effort to create democratic spaces, was a restriction against blacks "loitering about stores." Even though local government provided blacks the right to freely move throughout the public and private spaces, the mayor and alderman passed an ordinance that criminalized persons living in the city without gainful employment and labeled such persons "paupers and vagrants." The measure went so far as to punish people "knowingly and willfully bring [sic] or introducing into the city of Jacksonville any pauper or vagrant or any person not having the means to support him or her, and who is unwilling or unable to work or otherwise support himself or herself in a respectable way." Although this legislation was written to restrict blacks within the public and private spaces, the intent was to use this measure to control and order spaces the migrant blacks occupied when coming to the city from the countryside. The governor and constitutional delegates debated the same issue of "vagrancy" out of fear that blacks would leave the plantation belt for the port cities and be destitute due to lack of gainful employment. This measure did not make the final draft of the Florida Constitution of 1865 but did find its way to Jacksonville. Although there is no direct evidence of the impact of black mobilization in the public sphere to influence the passing of these ordinances, the right of African Americans to freely move about and assemble in the private and public spaces was central to codifying the idea that blacks too enjoyed democratized space.[6]

By the spring of 1867 the U.S. Congress introduced Military Reconstruction to the South, which abolished the former Confederate state governments constituted after the war. Southern states like Florida were assembled into military districts under the command of the U.S. Army. This provided hope that blacks could renegotiate the conditions and rights of citizenship lost in 1865. On May 25, 1867, local blacks took to the public space and organized a "Radical Union Republican" mass meeting. Black leaders feted the public space as they again organized their demands concerning the rights and privileges of black citizenship. This time the effort was not confined to the private spaces of the black churches, but was made public near the center of the city, demonstrating that under military authority blacks could organize openly and directly engage civil society as participants of the public. On stage and in the crowd were black as well as white residents all of whom engaged in a public discourse on the meaning of black equality, the franchise, and citizenship.

The Freedmen's Aid Society and the Ezekiel Band first marched through the city streets on their way to the groves on Julia Street, where a stage was erected for speakers. Over one thousand blacks were said to be in attendance. A committee, made up of prominent black men, presented a set of resolutions to the crowd to boisterous applause. The committee recognized that black men were "to assist in the reconstruction of the State under the new order of things" meant to describe the federal government taking an active role in reorganizing state and local governments. The committee declared that blacks would support the Republican Party due to its promotion of universal black male suffrage. The committee also introduced racial egalitarian principles such as the "education of the masses without distinction of color or race" and that blacks "have all the rights and privileges that belong to white citizens."[7]

The first speaker was an African American named Samuel Spearing. He declared himself an "American citizen," but questioned what that meant. He stated:

> under the law we are equal with the white man . . . [yet] we have not the right to sit in a jury box. On every jury there should be six white and six colored men. . . . we have a right to appointments on the police . . . the right to hold public offices . . . [and when] we have a right to a colored Justice of the Peace then we can shake hands with our white friends and say we have equal rights with them.[8]

Spearing expressed the sentiment of the crowd when he challenged the criticism that since white men owned the land and most of the wealth, they deserved to exclusively steer the government. He questioned: "how did they get the land and the wealth?" He replied to the crowd: "by the bone and sinew of the colored man."[9]

The meeting's purpose was to present local black voters with their political options, not candidates. Lucius Augustus Hardee, a captain in the Confederate Army, spoke out in support of the conservative or Democratic Party position. He opened by declaring that he knew "you colored people" because he "drew the first milk that strengthen[ed] his infant frame from the breast of a colored woman." He chastised blacks for their nostalgia of the abolitionists and their clothing of all Northern whites in the same abolitionist cause when most were not. He made the case that Northerners were the true political enemy to both Southern whites and blacks stating "I prefer a black negro to a Yankee to govern me." Hardee did not win the crowd over, many of whom yelled "colored" correcting him when he referred to them as "negro." When Hardee finally challenged the crowd to test Northerners' support for equality by asking the black men in attendance to marry the daughters of Northern whites this resulted in the crowd demanding he leave the stage. Horatio Bisbee, Jr., a local white Republican Party official, followed Hardee and warned against exclusively electing black officials as a plot by Southern whites to promote incompetent black office holders who could "prove" that blacks did not deserve the right to suffrage, a statement met with cheers by the crowd.[10]

Not only were black men engaging in the public political sphere, but also in the private political sphere as well. Integrated political organizations like the Union Republican Club met in private to organize electoral efforts. The Union Republican Club was run by prominent white men and had many black members. Throughout 1867 they met in secret in the Odd Fellows Hall organizing meetings and voter drives not only in the city but throughout other parts of the state. They probably organized the mass meeting of blacks since many who spoke were also members of the club. The club's constitution declared that "no distinction founded on race or color ought to abridge or any way interfere with the civil or political rights and privileges of any citizen." Additionally the club admonished the curbing of the free exercise of speech and assembly, which they claimed the local papers promoted. The club also hired lawyers to investigate claims leveled by local blacks who reported violations of their civil rights.[11]

Organizations like the Union Republican Club soon took to registering black voters. The *Florida Union* reported that 705 black men from Duval County were registered to vote by October 1867 representing 64 percent of voters since former Confederate officials and office holders were newly disfranchised by Military Reconstruction. The mobilization of blacks as a voting bloc led some local white residents to fear black male suffrage. One native white resident lamented "if the Negroes and their devilish white leaders prevail, I think we shall all go to the devil." Northern whites, however, were more optimistic. C. Thurston Chase, a white Northerner and former Freedmen's Bureau official, soon after the ratification of the 1868 Florida Constitution concluded, "[t]he success of the Repu [*sic*] ticket here & the ratification of the constitution by the people will secure a better day for Florida." After a contentious Constitutional Convention in February 1868, black men were formally given the right to vote. Conservative Republicans excluded radicals and passed a constitution that provided for suffrage rights to black men over the age of twenty-one, but restricted apportionment to no more than four representatives per county, so large counties with black majorities could not have a greater voice than smaller white majority counties—thus preserving majority white rule in Tallahassee. Additionally delegates empowered the governor to appoint many county and municipal office holders continuing to ensure white rule at the local level. The 1868 Florida Constitution did provide for the rights of all citizens without regard to race including speech and public assembly. The editor of the *Florida Union* praised the new constitution as extending "the right hand of fellowship" and welcoming blacks to "equal citizenship," while the Democratic Party offered nothing but "obsolete doctrines," "white man's government," and "a war of the races." Radical Republicans would have taken exception to the idea that the constitution challenged "white man's government" however.[12]

The 1868 Florida Constitution stipulated no "civil or political distinction" to any citizen regardless of race or previous condition of servitude. Although the state government pointed to equal treatment of blacks as a legal concept, in practice that was not always the case concerning private interactions in public space. By 1870 the state passed a law specifically demanding transportation companies grant access to their services to anyone willing and able to pay and additionally requiring equal access to all patrons inside facilities on steamships, stages, railroads, and all common carriers. In January 1873 this was followed by the Florida Civil Rights Law, which extended these same provisions for common carriers to hotels, theatres, parks, and schools. Private schools and cemeteries, which were funded without public monies, were excluded from these provisions.[13] Under the Florida Reconstruction, government citizens had equal access to all public space.

Michael Perman concludes that in the South during Reconstruction both the Republican and Democratic parties could not expect unity since each contained factions with divergent economic interest. These factions would conflict over the shape of the new political order during and after Reconstruction.[14] Republican unity would not only be tested with the 1868 Florida Constitution, but also through local elections. In the December

1868 election for U.S. Congress, Republicans in Duval County held a mass meeting at Hart's Grove to inform voters not to elect William U. Saunders, a black radical Republican, who ran against the moderate candidate under the "unterrified tiger committee." A racially integrated crowd listened to Republican leaders throughout the state, including Republican Governor Harrison Reed, endorse the reelection of Charles M. Hamilton, a white Northerner. A black Republican leader from Gainesville, Henry S. Harmon, even spoke to the crowd and declared "tiger skins were at a discount in this county." Republicans in northeast Florida feared an independent Republican candidate would sway the election to the Democrats, especially one as popular as Saunders.[15] Hamilton eventually won reelection easily. T. Frederick Davis recorded that while blacks mobilized for state and national elections throughout 1868 and 1869, it was not until April 1870 that black voters organized mass meetings to overturn Democratic rule in municipal elections. He reported that Peter Jones, a Northern transplant to the city, led these public meetings and won a slim victory over two-time mayor and Democrat Edward Hopkins. The *Tallahassee Weekly Floridian* declared that "Jacksonville has become completely Radicalized." The election would also touch off a visceral rhetoric of opponents declaring "dirty tricks" and "stuffing the ballot box" that both Democrats and Republicans would use to malign municipal elections throughout the end of the nineteenth century.[16]

What state and local elections in Duval County in 1869 and 1870 represent is the integration of black men into the public sphere. Although the political speech could get discursive in regard to candidates and policies, local blacks and whites could participate in the public and private spaces in ways not conceived before the war. The fact that white political leaders controlled many private and public spaces such as the Union Republican Club, the 1868 Constitutional Convention, and political meetings to elect white Republican candidates, blacks did participate in integrated settings to demonstrate that these spaces were more democratized. The ability of blacks to move through public and private spaces freely was a conscious right to black activists and politicians who helped to encode these rights into law as well as through their private organizations.

As the black elite and middle class were able to insert themselves into the public sphere, they were not the only segment of local African Americans to emerge into the new integrated public. The Civil War transformed the political culture of the city and the culture of work as well. Before the war most blacks were tied to the institution of slavery, and thus that system of bondage tied them as a workforce to local slaveholders. Although blacks could and often did resist their treatment as slaves, direct and overt challenges to slaveholders could be interpreted as insurrection and a challenge to white control. With spaces now more democratized than before the war and with the federal government as a presence through the local office of the Freedmen's Bureau, the black working class could engage the public sphere in similar ways as the black middle class. During this time black workers confronted the Freedmen's Bureau in order to force them to take a role in the negotiation of work and labor.

The Freedmen's Bureau witnessed and when necessary had to negotiate the transition of blacks to a wage-labor workforce. The Freedmen's Bureau was established initially as an agency within the U.S. Army to help former slaves and African Americans adjust to freedom in the South. The bureau set out to open schools and churches and eventually to find work for blacks so that they could be reintegrated into the postwar Southern economy. While reconciliation was slow between native whites and the federal presence throughout the city, labor disputes would draw the Freedmen's Bureau increasingly toward intervening into the working lives of African Americans.

The bureau's numerous duties included settling labor disputes between white employers and black employees. These incidents were usually adjudicated in the private spaces of the bureau offices. Robert C. Lowry, a Jacksonville agent with the bureau, was in charge of investigating and settling such disputes. In the spring of 1867, many blacks leveled a complaint against Frank Howard, who they claimed did not pay them their wages. After crossing out his threat to collect those wages directly, Lowry merely warned the planter that "if there are any more such complaints made substantiated," he would refer the matter to district headquarters. In another case Charles Alexander and Clarissa Stephens both claimed their employer M.H.G. Sandens abused them. Lowry asked Sandens to submit the name of "a distinguished citizen" who would inquire into the "facts" surrounding the incident and prepare a report with a recommendation to settle the case. Similar to the letter to Howard, Lowry crossed out his threat to "personally" deal with the planter if he did not follow through on this request.[17]

Many other cases, however, brought blacks out into the public spaces to engage the public sphere more openly. Andrew Mahoney used the offices of the Freedmen's Bureau to settle these issues more directly than Lowry. In his monthly reports during the spring and summer of 1867, Mahoney described a "growing evil" being thrust upon black domestic workers throughout the city. He claimed that many hotels and private residences would hire black workers as "servants," and before the end of the month when they were to collect their salaries these employers capriciously fired them without pay. He remorsefully noted that civil courts represented their only recourse, but since the financial onus to pursue the cases were on the plaintiffs, few blacks were successful in the ability to adjudicate these disputes and in most cases the court costs outstripped the financial claim. This had become such a problem that many blacks began to publicly protest, effectively striking before the end of the month, thus drawing the bureau's attention to the matter. Under the amorphous authority of the bureau, Mahoney claimed that most times he was successful in using his office as a location to settle these matters each month and secure the back pay owed by these employers.[18] By overseeing disputes—and at times quelling protests—black workers were successful in using the Freedmen's Bureau as an arm for advocacy and enforcement of their labor concerns.

Not all disputes were settled in the private spaces of the Freedmen's Bureau offices. One case in point occurred on the morning of 12 January 1867. A Florida labor agent recruited three hundred African Americans from Camden, South Carolina, to work on the plantations of Alachua County. They traveled on the steamer *Dictator* to the port in Jacksonville to later board a train for Gainesville. Upon their arrival, Mahoney learned that the labor recruiter never drew up contracts and all terms for work were communicated verbally. Mahoney believed that the terms by which these workers came to Florida held no apparent benefit to them and questioned whether they had been deceived or just "deluded" themselves. Mahoney then informed the three hundred plus workers that they were under no obligation to work without a written contract enforceable under state law. He told them they had the option to remain in Jacksonville to sell their labor to the highest bidder or to take the train with the recruiter on to Alachua County.

Throughout the day a rumor spread with local blacks that the recruiter's true intentions were to ship the passengers to Cuba and sell them into slavery. Mahoney reported that a mob of two hundred blacks came to the train station followed by the city marshal along with a posse. Mahoney

Figure 2. Florida, Atlantic and Gulf Central Railroad depot, Jacksonville, 1864. State of Florida Archives, Florida Photographic Collection.

stated that, "matters began to assume a serious character and had all the appearance of a Riot." Upon informing the restless crowd that the rumor was not true, he swung open the railroad doors to proclaim that all the workers inside had the "liberty" to leave or stay. He reported that approximately one hundred black workers decided to remain, while the rest departed for Gainesville.[19]

More often than not agents for the bureau felt they had to represent the best interest of black workers in disputes with white employers. When blacks aired their complaints in the public space, as in the cases of the protest at the railroad station or the striking domestic workers, the Freedmen's Bureau became more active in intervening and settling their disputes. Under the auspices of the federal government, black workers were able to individually and collectively engage in labor negotiations in the public and private spaces to demonstrate that democratized space was not a purview solely of the middle class.

Table 3. Total population of Duval County, 1860–1870

Year	Total	White	Percent (%)	Black	Percent (%)
1860	5,074	2,925	57	2,149	42
1870	11,921	5,141	43	6,780	56

Source: Historical Census Browser. Retrieved 4 March 2012 from the University of Virginia Geospatial and Statistical Data Center, http://www.fisher.lib.virginia.edu /collections/stats/histcensus/index.html.

The military and the federal presence in the city would not last indefinitely. Even though the military did not leave Jacksonville at the conclusion of the Civil War, the military was no longer composed primarily of African Americans since most black troops had been slowly mustered out of service and only white troops remained as arbitrators of the public spaces.[20] By 1869 the end of the Civil War had not settled many of the social problems born out of the conflict. Many African Americans had migrated to the city due to its economic expansion, thriving port, and booming saw mills.[21]

As the population of Jacksonville increased during this time, many of the black migrants who came were pushed out to the communities beyond the city limits such as La Villa and Brooklyn. According to reports, Brooklyn had become a haven for gambling, prostitution, and alcohol. White soldiers frequented these establishments where the only police force was the military. Conflicts between blacks living in Brooklyn and soldiers engaging in vices were common including stories that soldiers drove protesting residents out of the community periodically.[22] Questions about who controlled and policed the public spaces of these migrant black towns were in question since they were beyond the city limits.

Reports about the 1869 riot vary greatly. In letters to Edward Hopkins, the mayor of Jacksonville, Lieutenant Colonel C. C. Gilbert claimed that on the morning of 22 February, a number of black citizens from the Brooklyn section reported that soldiers were "behaving badly." Gilbert dispatched soldiers to patrol the streets of Brooklyn every thirty minutes to keep order throughout the evening and arrest any soldiers caught socializing there. Additionally Gilbert ordered two roll call inspections that evening to be sure all soldiers were either in camp or on patrol. The encampment was on the north side of McCoy's Creek, and Brooklyn was on the south side. When one patrol at ten in the evening tried to cross the bridge at McCoy's Creek to enter Brooklyn, roughly fifty African Americans were waiting with guns at the entrance of the bridge to Brooklyn. Gilbert reported that the patrol was fired upon while walking across the bridge and Private William Linehan, was mortally wounded.[23]

Captain Charles C. Raven, who commanded the patrol, noted that as the soldiers retreated, blacks lined up on the banks of the creek and fired into camp. Panicked, the patrol split into two groups. One group ran to La Villa, which bordered Brooklyn to the west, and the second group went north into town. Although he did not witness what happened, Raven claimed that when the second group entered the city they were fired upon by African Americans. He asserted that his men returned fire resulting in a black man being shot and a white tourist being wounded. Subsequently when Raven got to the city with several officers in tow they were able to quell the disturbance and return the soldiers back to camp.[24]

Observers reporting to local newspapers did not have the same impression of the riot. A reporter for the *Mercury and Floridian* concluded that the "riot (so-called)" was bore out of how poorly relations were between the white soldiers and local blacks. Relations were not only poor between the white soldiers and blacks, but also the soldiers and the former Confederates and their sympathizers who complained that they too were targets of harassment. Although the *Mercury and Floridian* reporter's name was anonymous, he did disclose he was a veteran of the Confederate Army. He went on to chastise the troops, who he said targeted any and all blacks in the city, while it was only "a few dissatisfied disaffected ones" who sought revenge on the soldiers. He concluded that "it was certainly not right . . . to proceed to this city for the purpose of making a general attack upon the race—upon innocent as well as guilty." The reporter implied that the soldiers involved lied in their official testimony when claiming they only fired on blacks who fired on them first.[25] Relations between the military and local blacks and native whites had gotten to the point that Southern whites were allied with blacks in protesting the military's policing of public spaces in and around the city.

The *Florida Union* stated that the reason the patrol went to the bridge on the evening of the 22nd was because they heard that a soldier had been shot in Brooklyn and went to investigate when they were ambushed by the black mob. The reporter then claimed that the sheriff followed after hearing the shots and dispersed the mob. According to the *Union* then the soldiers,

> advanced under orders and the officers dividing them into equals, ordered them to "charge upon the block and take every d——n nigger." Then the soldiers commenced a brisk fusillade firing rapidly and recklessly in every direction. Having soon cleaned out the "Rotten Row," as it is called, they marched through the principal streets, taking up every negro they met and firing at those who wouldn't stop and then returning to camp carrying about a dozen prisoners.[26]

One eyewitness reported that when he saw the soldiers attacking blacks on the streets, he asked the sheriff to restore order. To which the sheriff and police chief asked the commander to send his troops back to camp. By this point residents who were not apprised of the specific events assumed the military were putting down a "negro uprising," and welcomed the troops parading twenty wounded prisoners through the streets on their way back to camp.[27]

It is difficult to reconcile the varied reports of the riot. Part of the problem with the eyewitness testimonies is that no one person witnessed all of

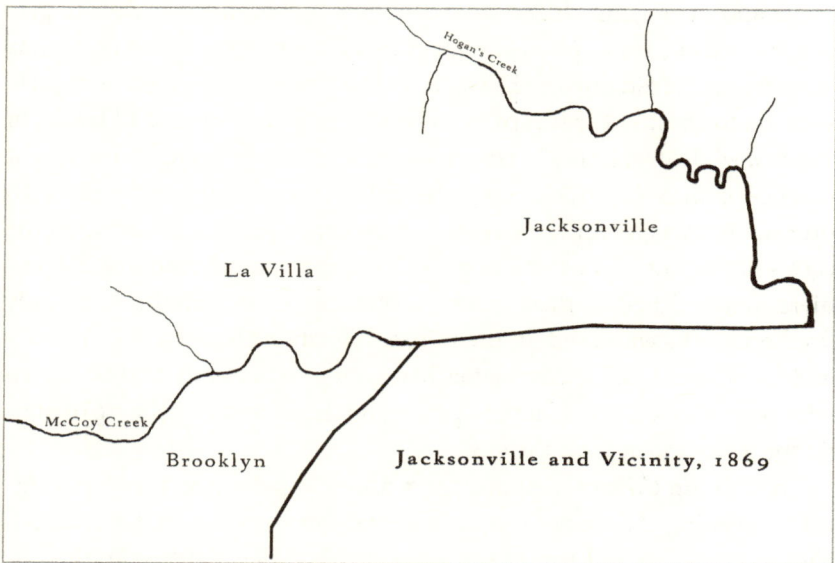

Figure 3. Map of Jacksonville and vicinity, 1869. Created by Anne Ladyem McDivitt.

the evening's events and instead relied upon other sources of information to fill in the gaps. One thing is clear: the presence of troops did create a common enemy for both blacks and native white residents. In Gilbert's report to the assistant adjutant general, he pointed out that he and his men recognized two groups: one "free from the taint of having been at any time identified with the public enemy, the other is practically regarded as not entirely free from that taint." He went on to state that Florida under Military Reconstruction was analogous to the experiences of Texas before statehood. As such, troops in territorial Texas were required "by law" to "maintain the upmost forbearance" toward the citizens (white settlers) of said territory. However, he argued an officer would be "derelict" if said officer did not "attack at once and push the affair with vigor" in the face of armed threat from the "public enemy (the Indians)." Gilbert postulated that in Jacksonville since blacks were the citizens and native-born whites were the "public enemy," he questioned what his officers should have done in the face of an armed attack by its citizens. He requested the government provide an answer to that question.[28]

City leaders did not stand idly by as the military investigated the riot. On 23 February a group of citizens held a meeting where they issued the following statement:

> That as citizens of Jacksonville, we all deplore such scenes of violence as wrong in themselves and injurious to the interests of the city, and we advise a calm reliance upon the administration of the law by the civil authorities. . . . We also, as law respecting citizens, will support the proper authorities in their investigation of law.[29]

Additionally, Captain Raven was arrested and fined for "breach of the peace within the city limits." Charges were eventually dropped by the state under the condition that the military pursue a full investigation. Soon after this, troops left Jacksonville and the city was turned over to civilian authorities.[30]

As with the Jacksonville Mutiny, the riot of 1869 was a resistance against how the military treated blacks in addition to native-born whites in the public spaces. This was a rejection of the military acting as the state. The 1860s turned out to be a period when blacks would enjoy access to democratized spaces unlike before. Local and state government fashioned legislation to define public and private spaces as equal regardless of race.

Within the environment of these democratized spaces blacks emerged from the private to the public spaces and politically engaged openly throughout the city. Blacks did not have to create a distinct or separate public sphere, but instead integrated themselves into the city's unitary public sphere. As the military left Jacksonville, blacks were participant citizens in civic life.

3

The Mob-Public

After the military moved out of Jacksonville in the winter of 1869, black men already inserted themselves into the Reconstruction Era public sphere. Under the guidance and cooperation of Northern white Republicans, blacks engaged civic life. Although the exit of the military signaled an end to Reconstruction, it did not immediately translate into the exclusion of black men from the public sphere. Throughout the last decades of the nineteenth century, the native white effort to push blacks out of the public sphere slowly evolved over time. Buttressed between the factionalism of both the Republican and Democratic parties, black voters and their local leaders could maneuver around the vulgar attempts by white reactionaries to reform electoral politics along the precepts of white supremacy and black exclusion. However, this détente would not last.

Throughout the 1870s and 1880s blacks could participate in the public sphere as long as their participation did not threaten white political supremacy and did not implicitly or explicitly suggest inherent racial equality between blacks and whites. As such, conservative whites recast black participation, even in integrated political settings, as a "mob-public" who enjoyed illegitimate access to the franchise and the public sphere itself. State and municipal elections became events interpreted by conservative whites almost as festival atmospheres where high political culture (white male voters) and low political culture (black male voters) joined together, the result of which was the vulgarization of the public sphere.[1] Conservative white politicians targeted white splinter candidates and factions who organized black voters in successful blocs as supporters. In these cases conservative white pols recast black voters as part of a mindless mob that was a cancer on the exalted system of representative democracy.[2]

Republicans and Democrats ran in local elections and at times vied for black votes throughout the 1870s. In the 1873 election a conservative Republican, J. C. Greeley, was elected through support in a coalition of conservative Republicans and Democrats. This factionalism was more pronounced during the 1876 municipal election, locally referred to as the return of "home rule." A conservative Republican named J. Ramsay Dey ran under the "Bolting Republican" ticket, as the *Florida Union* derisively called it. The Republicans did not have a monopoly on factionalism as the Democratic Party too was split between two candidates. Former mayor Edward Hopkins ran as a Democrat, presumably a native-born conservative Democrat and Luther McConihe ran as a Reform candidate and was regarded locally as a "good Boston Yankee." Edward C. Williamson referred to this split within the Democratic Party of Florida during this time as the rise of "independentism."[3] McConihe garnered 448 votes, while only 92 went to Hopkins. The totals for both Peter Jones, the Republican candidate, and Dey did not surpass McConihe alone. The election demonstrated that conservative Republicans probably crossed over to the Reform ticket, while Reformers held on to a majority of Democratic voters. Reform Democrats were elected down ticket except for the election of two conservative Republicans as aldermen. The Reform coalition held during the following election in 1877.[4]

Rather than being indicative of home rule, the 1876 election was the start of an era of fusion tickets. Conservative Republicans were not the only voting bloc up for grabs. It also represented the first evidence of black voters crossing political lines and voting for "reform Democrats." The *Daily Florida Union* reported that during the 1876 election, groups of "young Reformers" split from conservative or Bourbon Democrats. Local Bourbons pointed out that Reformers were meeting with a "negro

club"—presumably a black Republican organization. One Bourbon observer stated that "a negro club and its delegate [were] received with open
arms" by "Radicals, who were laughing at us in their sleeves." From this
meeting the black club agreed to organize votes for the Reform candidate with a black Republican selected as alderman on the same ticket.
Bourbons interpreted this event as the subversion of Democratic Party
principles and a threat to democracy itself. Bourbons pointed out that the
state and national Democratic parties rigidly promoted white supremacy
and the exclusion of blacks from party membership. Black delegates were
referred to repeatedly as the "enemy" and black politicians as "objection-
able." Bourbons argued that "no one owes allegiance to a heterogeneous
mass, although styled a 'reform meeting,' with 'Democratic principles' as
its basis." In the minds of local Bourbons, the fact that black men shared
the same space as Reform Democrats created an atmosphere where "no
reform could be secured except by the practical discarding of Democratic
principles."[5] Although Bourbons believed that black male voters represented a lower order or "mass," they placed blame for this interracial political meeting squarely on Reform Democrats, who they believed were
unscrupulous.

Black political leaders held out hope that opportunities like this to
cross party lines gave black voters leverage and voice in local elections.
Longtime black Republican stalwart, John R. Scott, even lamented after
the 1877 election:

> Negroes will not complain if greater protection for life and property
> and educational advances are secured as promised by the Demo-
> crats during the campaign. . . . negro voters . . . will always co-oper-
> ate with that party which acknowledges his manhood and respects
> his right to an equal chance with the Anglo-Saxon race.[6]

Throughout this time, black voters would help play an electoral pivot for
fusion tickets and Reform candidates. African American delegates still
represented Jacksonville in district and state Republican meetings and
conventions. In county elections, where African Americans constituted a
significant majority of qualified voters, blacks helped elect white Republicans to the U.S. Congress and black representatives to the state Constitutional Convention in 1885.[7]

What transpired on the local level replicated itself statewide. In addition, Bourbon Democrats targeted black voters as a way to minimize

electoral support for Reform Democrats. During the administration of Governor William Bloxham, Bourbon Democrats were attacked by "independent" Democrats who believed Bloxham and other Bourbons were too cozy to big business, the railroads, and real estate developers like Hamilton Disston. Independent Democrats were reportedly from the rural parts of Florida and not connected to the "Tallahassee Ring." Adding to this political discontent was the 1868 Florida Constitution, which created a strong governor and not only left the very few black majority counties without a local voice but also all the majority white Democratic counties.

Statewide, Bourbons and independents fought bitterly in the 1884 election with the issue of a new constitution at the center of their dispute. In the general election of that year, 74 percent of voters supported a referendum demanding a new constitution, and as a result in 1885 the legislature held a Constitutional Convention. This movement to challenge Bourbon rule created a space for black politicians to have a seat at the table. Black Republicans joined the ranks of the "independent movement" by organizing a statewide conference in Gainesville on 5 February 1884 to support Independent Democrats. In return, black delegates to the conference demanded support for black public education, an end to the local mechanisms for disfranchising black votes, as well as eliminating racial discrimination on public transportation. Delegates were overwhelmingly Democrats with a small number of Republicans and an even smaller number of blacks elected. The greatest changes delegates introduced to the constitution that impacted black voting was the poll tax and clothing the governor with the power to only appoint county commissioners, leaving municipal officials to local elections.[8]

Different constituencies objected to the poll tax. Thomas V. Gibbs, a black delegate from Jacksonville, openly rejected the poll tax and many of the changes that impacted the franchise in the new Florida Constitution. Michael Perman has noted that throughout the South, Democratic politicians from black belt counties usually were reluctant to sign off on disfranchisement efforts because they wanted the opportunity to harness the mass of black voters.[9] Gibbs claimed that Bourbons were conservative Democrats from "black belt" counties who wished to maintain electoral hegemony over the black majorities in their districts. He observed that liberals (or Reformers) were Northern whites who were at one time conservative Republicans, but the color line drove them into the Democratic Party. Gibbs explained that liberal Democrats fought with Bourbon Democrats to keep the poll tax out of the new constitution, but Bourbon intransigence wore them down and liberals eventually gave into the poll tax on the tacit agreement that the legislature could have the power to enforce it but would not. One victory Gibbs pointed to was the change in the court system whereby the justice-of-the-peace courts would be elected instead of appointed. Gibbs hoped that would eliminate the local court system as a mechanism for black voter disfranchisement. Gibbs claimed that these courts were "a wholesale disfranchising machine to disqualify blacks. About 3,000 voters for trivial offences or on trumped up charges have been disfranchised. This, under the proposed constitution, if ratified, will be stopped, as only courts of record can impose penalties which carry with them disfranchisement."[10]

In return for this concession Bourbons received appointed circuit court judges and county commissioners, which gave a Democratic governor the power to select the people in charge of running and enforcing policies for local elections. Gibbs concluded that these compromises demonstrated that Bourbon Democrats distrusted fair and free elections because they prevented "any mandatory constitutional provision for the protection and purity of the ballot."[11]

For Bourbons or conservative Democrats, removing blacks from the franchise as a "mass" of voters represented a reform of elections. J. J. Daniel, a Jacksonville Bourbon, declared that "negroes as a class were recognized to be ignorant and easily led astray by designing political tricksters." According to Daniel the "tricksters" were "young" Democrats who he suggested were no better than Reconstruction era Republicans. Daniel threw his support to the 1885 Florida Constitution because he believed the poll tax would remove immigrants, blacks, and poor whites as temptations for Reform or Independent Democrats to make political mischief.[12]

Edwin M. Randall, a white delegate from Jacksonville, submitted a petition from the Florida Mechanics and Workingmen's Association of Jacksonville created through a convention of the "working people" at Livingston Hall on West Forsyth Street. The Workingmen's Association was a racially integrated organization but with segregated chapters; thus, this could have provided for the private space by which blacks and working-class whites could find common cause. The resolution proclaimed the poll tax "savors too much of aristocracy and despotism" and circumvents the free exercise of working people's citizenship rights.[13]

What the 1885 Constitutional Convention did was create a political alliance among white labor, Reform Democrats, and black voters. The alliance was obvious in the debates concerning education and the franchise. At the convention Gibbs introduced a provision for the creation of a black and white normal school to train teachers, and Randall introduced language to the Florida Constitution requiring that "impartial provision shall be made for the instruction of white and colored children in public schools." Both groups saw themselves as targets of the impending poll tax. Between August 1885 and February 1886 the Workingmen's Association met publicly to praise the delegates who voted against the poll tax at the convention. During a public meeting on 15 February 1886, the association formally presented Austin S. Mann, a delegate from Hernando County, with a gold badge for his emphatic denunciation of the poll tax. In an inscription on the badge the Workingmen's Association proclaimed, "He defended American Suffrage in the State Constitutional Convention, 1885," on the back they inscribed, "The voice of all the people is the voice of God."

By 1886 laborers in the city—both skilled and unskilled—had begun to organize and engage the public sphere. During this same time the white editor of the *Florida Times-Union* admonished the black editors of the local press for organizing blacks to vote as a bloc, much the same way the Workingmen's Association was starting to do by 1886.[14] Although Bourbons were adamant in their desire to quell the black vote and remove blacks from the public sphere, political alliances and bloc voting saved blacks from the most extreme electoral reforms pushed by conservative Democrats during the 1885 Constitutional Convention.

In the municipal elections of 1886, political fractures within the Democratic Party would again come to a head. The political alliances born out of the 1885 Florida Constitution would translate to political victories locally in 1886. The Young Men's Democratic Club nominated John Q. Burbridge for mayor, while the city's Democratic Convention nominated William Mclaws Dancy. Charles H. Jones, editor of the *Florida Times-Union* supported Burbridge and the Young Democrats. Jones defended them from charges of being "Bolters." The Republicans ran no candidate, and Burbridge declined participating in the primary. Jones criticized the primary system and claimed that "[i]f the candidate of the better classes of citizens goes into them with his friends, they are out-numbered and out-voted by the riff-raff and rabble that can always be relied upon to turn out in full force at the call of the bosses."[15]

Duncan U. Fletcher who was president of the Young Men's Democratic Club during this election expressed concerns that the Democratic primary system did not represent the will of the "Democratic majority." In response Fletcher stated the club was taking "an earnest effort to lend their aid toward purifying our city politics and in doing so, began at the fountain head of disorder." The so-called fountain head of disorder was the primary system reportedly run by entrenched regular Democrats who the club hoped to circumvent, win the general election, and reform the political system so "an honest and fair expression of the Democratic majority can be had." The club referred to regular Democrats as "city bosses" who turned out voters through their machines much like Tammany Hall in New York City during this same time. The Reformers that made up the club demanded not only an end to machine politics but also efficient tax collection, cleaner streets, paid fire departments, along with other public improvements.[16]

At the Democratic primary meetings held in each of the four wards, Dancy emerged unanimous. In the fourth ward reporters described it as "a regular old fashioned Republican convention." Blacks and whites were said to be rowdy—their behavior prompted a number of people to leave. Some witnesses charged that the meeting was high-jacked by "a few drunken negroes and parties who had no legal right to participate in a Democratic primary meeting." Dancy's opponents claimed that the events in the fourth ward were orchestrated by his supporters who wanted to silence opposition through the "turbulence of a mob." Burbridge's supporters soon after organized a political meeting to offer voters a "Citizens' Ticket." During the April municipal election the *Florida Times-Union* charged Dancy with purchasing votes "as openly and shamelessly as cattle in a cattle market." Citizens' Ticket supporters also claimed that saloon men and a handful of political operatives were in control of the local Democratic Party and could bring out the "lawless, vicious and vagrant elements" to mobilize on Election Day.[17]

The Citizens' Ticket organized blacks, Republicans, labor, and disaffected Democrats as a voting bloc. Reform leaders claimed that if more cross sections of the population participated, the handful of men that ran municipal elections would be challenged. The *Southern Leader*, one of the local black newspapers, helped to organize blacks to support the Citizens' Ticket. In his victory speech Burbridge declared that if not for black voters, "the opposition would have overridden us." Burbridge also promised:

> I shall know no one on account of his color and I shall make no distinctions. The colored man can get justice from me as well as the white. Whenever he deserves it I shall do him justice. Why? Because they have rallied around us in this fight and saved us from a government not of the people, but of a clique.[18]

H. H. Baker and Mose Taylor, two black organizers for the Citizens' Ticket, serenaded Burbridge after the speech, and the mayor publicly invited them into his home for refreshments to symbolically show the new place for blacks in local politics. Thomas V. Gibbs was even cautiously optimistic when declaring in a letter to the *New York Freeman* in July 1887 that in Jacksonville "color disadvantages are gradually lessening . . . in business relations, rapidly; in political relations steadily; in religious and social relations very slowly." The reason for caution was because of how tenuous black participation in this new political coalition was. An editorial from the *Florida Times-Union* implied that black leaders could have a seat at the table as long as the "intelligent" class could deliver the black masses away from the "gamblers and liquor men" who would "come down with enough boodle" to bid on "the votes of the depraved and ignorant."[19]

In keeping with their campaign promise to clean up municipal elections, the newly elected mayor and city council incorporated the black suburbs of LaVilla and Fairfield, adjacent to East Jacksonville and Oakland, which increased the black vote to a slim majority of 364 registered black voters over white voters. Although the politicians elected under the Citizens' Ticket sought the black vote, they remained apprehensive of the electoral influence of a black majority. As they incorporated the black suburbs, the local government also decreased the power of the mayor to that of a virtual figurehead and shifted the responsibility of city management to the city council. In addition, they changed the voting districts within the city to elect candidates from each ward instead of at large elections. The new city charter created nine ward districts, and in only three there would be a slight African American voting majority so that black voters en masse could never elect a majority of officials on the city council. As a result of coalition politics and careful restructuring of the city charter,

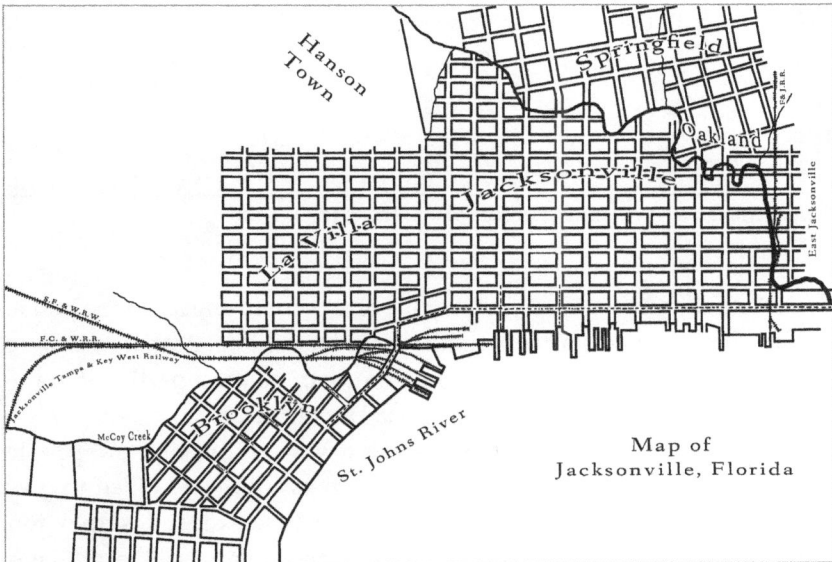

Figure 4. Map of Jacksonville, 1884. Created by Anne Ladyem McDivitt.

local government would still be primarily controlled by whites—but black leaders would have a seat at the table.[20]

The Citizens' Ticket coalition and the eventual restructuring of the city's voting districts brought Republicans back into local politics. After incorporating the suburbs and dividing the city into multiple wards, local residents in the areas affected by this change demanded a new election. Mass meetings were held in each of the wards to select candidates for a straight ticket on the December 1887 election. Democrats, Republicans, blacks, and white labor candidates were chosen through this process. Charles B. Smith, a Republican, was at the head of the ticket as a candidate for mayor and promoted as a conservative businessman while candidates for alderman rounded out the rest of the ticket. Nine Republicans were selected, five of whom were black. An equal number of Democrats as Republicans were selected with ten of the candidates from both parties being members of the Knights of Labor. Blacks, Democrats, Republicans, and union members met independently to select candidates with "workingmen" in LaVilla, hosting the only interracial nominating meeting. Late into the election, a group of dissenters supported an opposition ticket called the Union Ticket that also drew from disaffected regular Democrats, blacks, and Republicans and selected Frank W. Pope at the top of

Table 4. Total population of Jacksonville, 1870–1890

Year	Total	White	Percent (%)	Black	Percent (%)
1870	6,912	2,923	42	3,989	57
1880	7,650	3,991	52	3,658	47
1890	17,201	7,372	42	9,801	56

Source: Bureau of the Census, *Census of Population*, 1870–1890.

the ticket. This demonstrated that while blacks could engage in the public sphere, their political participation was not monolithic. Both tickets were nonpartisan and had representatives from both political parties with the Union Ticket made up of mostly regular Democrats.

Union Ticket meetings were disasters with reportedly few people showing up—including the prominent citizens who were billed to give endorsements. However, like some Citizens' Ticket meetings, they too were integrated. Union Ticket organizers placed some black candidates on their tickets—many of whom summarily bolted for the Citizens' Ticket. With this victory, African American voters were rewarded with appointments on the police force, an African American selected to the police commission, and another as a judge of the municipal court. This represented the first time since Reconstruction that African Americans played such an influential role in local politics. This newfound participation and association with labor would soon end and ring in a different era.[21]

While the election of the Citizens' Ticket went smoothly in December, it took months and the intervention of the Florida Supreme Court for the newly elected candidates to take office and select their appointees. Smith's opponents charged that the city purposely created confusion on Election Day to hamper the vote, and Smith had to sue in court to take office. In the summer of 1888 Jacksonville was hit with an epidemic of yellow fever. Between August and October 1888, the city lost a majority of its population to the disease or through flight. Mostly whites left including those in municipal government. White residents who remained complained that white majority control of municipal government was threatened.[22]

Daniel S. D. Belliny, a black resident of the city, was distraught at the ways in which the crisis became a critical charge against blacks. He stated that most whites had fled except for a number of white pastors who joined with black pastors to provide relief to those that remained. He challenged the newspaper coverage by stating unequivocally that roughly five thousand black laborers, not "loafers," roamed the streets because business owners and white government officials left. Belliny predicted a Republican victory in the upcoming November elections. He stated that there were still divisions within the Democratic Party because "the Farmers Alliance and the Knights of Labor are stinging thorns in their side." Additionally Belliny speculated that those that were leaving Jacksonville and northeast Florida were Democrats, so Republicans could pick up not only Duval County but the surrounding counties as well as far south as Volusia County. He concluded that the only drawback was that black access to public spaces were limited due to the fact that "people here and other infected districts, are prohibited from congregating in convention or mass meeting." Although Belliny was optimistic of the coming election for Republicans, he suspected the events would play out like a Shakespearean tragedy that "despite the scourge, the average Florida politician like Banquo's ghost, will not down, but poses in the hands of his friends."[23]

In the November 1888 election for county offices, a *Florida Times-Union* headline complained "No Show for Good, Honest Government Any More—A Sad Commentary on Unlimited Suffrage." The tenuous coalition of blacks and white reformers could not withstand the yellow fever epidemic. Working-class black women were the targets of criticism as well. The local papers blamed black women for creating a disturbance at the polling stations by "circulating around among their sable companions of the opposite sex, admonishing them to vote the 'publican ticket straight,' while others were content to sit on the opposite side of the street and watch [the] proceedings with manifest interest." The *Florida Times-Union* claimed that white voters were rare while "motley crowd[s] of negroes loaded to the muzzle with "stright [*sic*] 'Publican tickets." The *Times-Union* implied that left to their own devices, the black masses would vote Republican rather than the nonpartisan reform tickets. This was perceived to be an abandonment of the Citizens' Ticket agreement. Years later the *Florida Times-Union* would charge the "respectable class" of blacks of having no control of the black masses. And thus a majority of black voters left the nonpartisan coalition for a straight Republican ticket nullifying the tenuous alliance between black political leaders and reform Democrats. Democrats referred to the black masses that came from the suburbs to engage in the public sphere and vote during this time as "the colonizers," suggesting that they were outside the native body politic.[24]

The local press ran letters from citizens and visitors who were alarmed that blacks were so visible. One New York tourist claimed that, "for the first time, also I saw blue coated colored policemen." Local citizens also voiced their displeasure at the new role African Americans enjoyed, one complaining that "[h]ere in Jacksonville, where ninety-nine hundredths of our visitors and immigrants are white men, two-thirds of the 'guardians of the city's welfare,' are negroes!" A petition by "Five Ladies of Jacksonville" accused local blacks of making white "ladies" targets when they reported being "elbowed off the sidewalks by negroes walking three abreast and defiantly refusing to give an inch of the way." In each of these cases the *Florida Times-Union* connected these public disorders with black participation in municipal politics, reminding citizens of when during Reconstruction "the solid black mass of newly enfranchised ignorance and impudence defeated every measure for the welfare of the States." Glenda Elizabeth Gilmore concluded that in North Carolina during this same time, rural white women who migrated to the cities often used a lack of deference on the part of blacks as a threat to their perception as "ladies." Thus whites connecting blacks as a "mass" or people also would assume they too were the catalyst of social and political disorder.[25]

Those who joined in the campaign were united in the goal to take the vote and political influence away from African Americans. The *Florida Times-Union* effort to characterize how blacks acted in the city was intended to convince the state legislature that a serious social crisis existed in Florida's burgeoning flagship city. Local residents opposed to these measures labeled local whites who joined in this campaign as "dirty shirters."[26] The dirty shirters were able to get the state legislature to investigate the local "electoral crisis."[27] By April 1889, disfranchiser supporters depicted their local government, as well as city life, in disarray because of the active participation of the black masses in civic politics. Those counter to this movement claimed that the disfranchisers were taking democracy away from all of the citizens. The disfranchisers supported a bill that would allow the governor to appoint the mayor and the city council. They claimed that this measure was democratic, since voters elected the governor in the way voters elected the president of the country.[28]

Disfranchisers cried that they wanted "responsible" control of city government. Before the state legislature would vote on this measure, the state senate nominated a four-member committee to travel to Jacksonville to

witness the validity of the claims first hand. In response the local government gave all blacks on the police force the day off, so African Americans
would not be as visible during the committee's visit. The disfranchisers
then had the committee extend their stay. The committee returned to the
capital and recommended that the legislature revise the city charter to
give power to the governor to appoint the mayor and city council. They
concurred with the disfranchisers that the black voting mass in the city
were not responsible enough to elect a "fair" government; thus to ensure
that a "representative" government existed in the city, the state needed to
support the new charter bill.[29]

While there were many blacks who objected to the measure, some
blacks seemed to support the disfranchisers. Dating back to the yellow
fever epidemic, Belliny charged the Colored Auxiliary Bureau with helping to feed local white newspapers with stories of black depravity during the crisis. A similar charge was made against Frederick Douglass, the
famed black abolitionist, when he visited the city. In a speech on 5 April
1889, while admonishing the reported behavior of the black masses, Douglass declared that, "It will not do to claim for ourselves equality with the
whites in everything." He continued that "[i]t is no use for us, because
we can smoke cigars and block the sidewalks so that the white man cannot pass, for us to claim equality. . . . [t]hat is not equality." The *Florida
Times-Union* claimed that "the most reputable and self-respecting colored
people" were against the "self-assertive Black Guard Brigade." Emanuel
Fortune Jr., brother of T. Thomas Fortune, editor of the *New York Age,*
charged Douglass with providing cause for whites to attack blacks with
a specious claim. Fortune challenged him by stating that "Mr. Douglass
should know that when sidewalks are blocked in the South it is usually
by white people." This brought back the earlier charges the *Times-Union*
made against black women who confronted white "ladies" on the streets.
Fortune was not only calling out Douglass as aiding the local white press
in manipulating those events but also stating the accusations were wholly
fictitious and only spoke to how whites treated blacks. One white specta-
tor concluded that "the only fault he found with Douglass was that he was
too white for a colored man."[30]

The policy measure to address the "disorder" in Jacksonville was introduced to the legislature as House Bill Number Four. As the state legislature acted, local leaders took notice to how other large cities with

significant black populations dealt with similar problems. The Tennessee state legislature allowed the cities of Memphis, Nashville, Knoxville, and Chattanooga to utilize the Australian ballot system, or multiple ballot system, along with a literacy test to help disqualify a majority of black voters. With the Australian ballot, coupled with the literacy tests, it would be difficult to vote without having the ability to read and comprehend complex directions. This would effectively disqualify the black masses and white working class within the city. The local press supported the House bill as a temporary measure, and declared that given time, if the Tennessee system were proven successful in disfranchising the black vote, then the *Times-Union* recommended that Florida seriously consider a similar policy.[31]

A coalition of Democrats and conservative Republicans in the state legislature passed the House bill, which eventually made its way to Governor Francis P. Fleming's desk by the summer of 1889. The *Tampa Journal*, a Republican newspaper, voiced its opposition to the bill to no avail. The governor signed the bill as soon as he was assured it was constitutional and quickly selected eleven Democrats and seven Republicans to the city council. Opponents tried to fight the constitutionality of the bill and were denied a hearing before the Florida Supreme Court. Soon other communities in Florida with significant black voting majorities, like Palatka, petitioned the state legislature for a similar reorganization of their city charters. While House Bill Number Four temporarily placated the conservative element of Jacksonville, the new city charter was merely a temporary measure until an adequate system of disfranchisement could be established.[32]

Emanuel Fortune Jr. claimed that the legislative takeover of city government was a coup by conservative Democrats crying "we want no Negro domination. . . . we want white man's government." He observed that "Negro domination" resulted in white Republican government, and in no time in the city's history was there a black majority elected to office. Fortune concluded that black voters were being punished for electing Republicans in 1888. He charged Governor Fleming and U.S. Senator Wilkinson Call, both Jacksonville natives, with leading the coup to guarantee conservative Democratic rule on behalf of local party officials. No matter how debilitating this effort was to local blacks, Emanuel Fortune was optimistic in the long-term movement to secure black citizenship rights.[33] He warned:

What the South needs to do is to accord to all men their rights as citizens. This will have to be done sooner or later, because there are forces in operation which will in the future command this and the sooner the South does it the better it will be for it and for all concerned.[34]

Fortune suggested that the movement to secure the rights of blacks in the South would not diminish over time and would eventually overtake the conservative white position on race relations.

Quickly the local press and conservative politicians who supported this measure went on the defensive. Local newspapers responded to Northern critics that they did not understand what the South had gone through during the Reconstruction years. They claimed they did not want to return to a period dominated by black Republicans and so-called carpetbaggers. They also claimed that blacks in the South, specifically Jacksonville, were treated better than they were treated in Northern cities like Boston, New York, and Chicago. While this exchange appeared in the press, Jacksonville also began to vigorously advertise itself as a destination point for Northern travelers. The local press claimed no race problems existed and that the city was completely recovered from the yellow fever epidemic. This showed that by 1890, with the black vote no longer a factor, the city could try to become a destination again for Northern business and visitors—as it had been before the epidemic years and machine government.[35]

The notion of blacks representing a "mob-public" did not end with the revised city charter of 1889. The sizable black population, especially after the yellow fever epidemic of 1888, meant that black votes could be vied for in intraparty political disputes. Throughout the 1890s conservative Democrats chipped away around the edges in election policies to limit and quiet the voice of blacks in the public sphere. These efforts too caught popularity even within independent factions of the state Democratic Party, so that by the end of this period blacks were pushed out of the public sphere all in the name of electoral reform.

By the end of 1890, the conservative element of Jacksonville began the second phase of disfranchisement. They requested a repeal of the charter bill, which they had demanded so adamantly in 1889. An editorial in the *Florida Times-Union* stated: "[t]he dangers which then confronted us have been averted and a steadily growing public sentiment in favor of adoption of the Australian ballot system in this city and state makes it plain that we no longer have anything to fear from an elective municipal government in Jacksonville." Proponents now wanted the state legislature to utilize the Australian ballot system and poll tax as practiced in Tennessee. With those measures in place, conservatives believed the city charter remedy would be obsolete.[36]

The Straightouts would be the next phase of political reformers to "clean up" city government. Many of the old Citizens' Ticket leaders like Duncan U. Fletcher were part of this movement. It got its start in April during the 1892 County Democratic Convention. Straightouts became disillusioned with the charter solution to municipal government. Opponents claimed that in 1891 Mayor Henry Robinson formed an interracial coalition that petitioned the governor and legislature for local appointments—some of them going to blacks and Republicans. According to the *Florida Times-Union*, included in this coalition were black leaders, Republicans, laborers, and saloon keepers who were interested in lobbying Tallahassee and the state Democratic Party. The Straightouts emerged in 1892 to demand a "straight Democratic ticket." The *Times-Union* referred to supporters of the current system derisively as "Mahoneites," after the Virginia legislator William Mahone who formed a reform coalition in that state known as "Readjusters" that included blacks and Republicans. In the early 1880s they wrested control of the state from Bourbons along with the rhetoric of being "color blind," much like the Citizens' Ticket years earlier. The Straightouts would confront the "Mahoneites" at the Duval County Democratic Convention being held at Park Opera House.[37]

At the county convention, Straightouts challenged the Democratic primary election returns that selected delegates from each ward. Straightouts and other opponents of the current municipal regime read out the names of people who voted that were not registered Democrats but were Republicans or had no political affiliation. Previous to this election, officials did not authenticate a voter's registration. The Straightouts claimed they had hard evidence of voter fraud including people voting more than once and in wards where they were not residents. A majority of delegates agreed and empaneled a credentials committee to determine whether the delegates to the state convention could stand. The credentials committee moved for a new election, but the "Mahoneites" refused to give up their seats as state delegates. The meeting was said to be rowdy, which the

Florida Times-Union blamed on the "Mahoneites." Their intransigence at the meeting earned them the nickname "the Opera House Mob." Again black participation in the public sphere and political culture amounted to a "mob-public." The Straightouts convinced the Executive Committee to hold a new election on May 19th, where voters could be checked against an official registration list.[38]

One article in the *Florida Times-Union* went so far as to suggest that "the Mahoneite municipal government in this city has arraigned itself against law and order and is hand in glove with the rum sellers and keepers and patrons of disorderly resorts." The night before the election, prominent Straightouts gave speeches to the executive committee including Duncan U. Fletcher, John M. Barrs, and Napoleon Bonaparte Broward. Barrs stated that the opponents of the new primary "tried by every means possible to frustrate the plans of true democrats [*sic*] to rid the city of republican [*sic*] and negro rule." The *Times-Union* professed that "Mahoneism will be killed for all time in Duval County and the democratic masses will continue to control the actions of their party." On Election Day, opponents of the new primary were said to stay home as protest and not recognize the election. Additionally the *Times-Union* reported that "Mahoneites" recorded the names of workers who came out to vote and went to their employers to blacklist them. Straightouts won the election handily. Not everyone was a supporter of either side however. Louis Brush, who lived in a part of the city recently incorporated in 1887, complained about the factionalism in a letter to the *Florida Times-Union*. He said the fight over the primary was between two "aristocratic" factions, while voters like him were disfranchised under the new charter. Being denied the right to vote in city elections, he concluded:

> [I]n county affairs you can exercise your American manhood; in city affairs you are a "bump on a log." You can't vote—"taxation without representation." Throw the tea overboard."

Brush's revolt notwithstanding, the Straightouts moved to reform elections by lobbying the state legislature before the 1893 election.[39]

The Straightouts were successful in convincing the state legislature to incorporate the Australian ballot system, a poll tax measure, and a repeal of the House charter bill. Since the previous municipal government was associated with "disorder," during the 1893 election the public spaces in and around the polling stations were strictly policed. In the sweeping reforms passed by the legislature, people were banned from standing or assembling within fifty feet of a polling station and required that "no person shall speak to another" while in the "polling place." There was still a Citizen's Ticket coalition made up of liberal Republicans and white labor, which the paper referred to as the "Fusionists." In 1893, the Australian ballot system and poll tax effectively diluted the black vote. Straightout voters elected the mayor and twelve city council men, while their opponents the Fusionists, made up of labor, blacks, and Republicans, were only able to elect four city council men. There remained one ward, the sixth ward, that had a majority black voting base that was able to elect one councilman during this election. The Straightouts did not abandon black votes altogether, but hired blacks to speak at black political meetings to persuade them to vote for their candidates. According to James Weldon Johnson, using blacks to speak to black meetings was not a successful political strategy.[40]

This first phase of disfranchisement targeted the black masses. From 1893 through 1907, voters in the black sixth ward were able to elect a black city councilman, and at the turn of the century two black city councilmen represented the sixth ward. The new voting measures significantly reduced the numbers of the black masses. The black elite of Jacksonville could read and understand the complex instructions accompanying the Australian ballot, in addition to being able to afford the poll tax. Although Jacksonville's black elite did not support these disfranchisement measures, they were not restricted personally from the vote as indicated by the number of black officials elected to the city council between 1893 and 1907.[41] The black middle class sent representatives to the state capital to lobby against the change in voting regulations, but failed. Since they found little sympathy for their effort, they went back to the city and helped educate the voting masses on the specifics of the Australian ballot and continued participating in civic life as they had done throughout this period. The black middle class believed, or at least hoped, that this disfranchisement movement would eventually end. Conservative whites hoped that without the black working class voting, the black middle class would quietly disappear from civic life.[42]

Without large numbers of voters, black participation in coalition politics soon faded. White Republican politicians and officials would regularly campaign in the sixth ward, as did politicians who supported labor interest. These efforts were a shadow of the days of the Citizen's Ticket

Figure 5. Political cartoon from the *Sun* criticizing the "Colored Section" of the *Metropolis* newspaper, 6 January 1906. Library of Congress, *Chronicling America: Historic American Newspapers*.

coalition, since a majority of elected officials throughout this period were conservative Democrats. When labor, reform Democrats, and Republicans joined with the black vote they could succeed in an upset as in the 1895 election when these factions campaigned and a Republican was elected mayor. But this effort did not last through subsequent elections. Even though many blacks still voted, they did not always support a united effort or the same candidates. Judge Joseph Lee for example, a stalwart of the Republican Party in Florida, occasionally voted and campaigned for white conservative Republican candidates in the sixth ward, while others choose to directly oppose him. On election days, black leaders would sponsor rallies in the sixth ward to educate voters about the strict rules concerning the voting process. Labor would do the same in the predominantly white working-class wards; this suggests that the effort to disfranchise included working-class whites as well as blacks. In similar fashion, the local press complained that the element susceptible to graft was present throughout the city. This included the white as well as black wards. Although this change in voting procedure hindered much of the black vote, it did not extinguish black participation during local elections.[43]

During the 1870s and 1880s, black voters and black leaders in Jacksonville did openly engage and organize within the public sphere. Factional politics created the space for blacks to be integrated within the public sphere albeit through the paternalism of Independent Democrats and the "safeguards" of white majority governing. Throughout this time conservative Democrats challenged the atmosphere of an integrated public sphere as not only a betrayal of democratic principles but also holding the public sphere hostage to a "mob-public." A political discourse could exist and thrive even with black participation as long as it resulted in white majority government. As the yellow fever epidemic of 1888 created the conditions to challenge this tradition, white local leaders went to extreme measures to reduce the impact of black political participation.

4

The Black Counterpublic Emerges

As blacks were slowly pushed out of the public sphere in the 1880s and 1890s, a black counterpublic emerged. Initially the black counterpublic did not organize around politics or political parties but were concerned with questions surrounding the public safety of black suspects in the criminal justice system and the vigor with which the state protected them from lynching. As Nancy Fraser reminds us, a counterpublic serves a very important function not only to subaltern populations who organizes within it but also to the greater public sphere itself. Fraser concludes:

> In stratified societies, subaltern counterpublics have a dual character. On the one hand, they function as spaces of withdrawal and regroupment; on the other hand, they also function as bases and training grounds for agitational activities directed toward wider publics. . . . This dialectic enables subaltern counterpublics partially to offset, although not wholly to eradicate, the unjust participatory privileges enjoyed by members of dominant social groups in stratified societies.[1]

As black men were moved out of the public sphere and their voices in political culture were being silenced, a counterpublic evolved to broadly and narrowly question the legal rights of blacks within a racially stratified society.

Extralegal violence hung over Jacksonville like a specter at the close of the Civil War. In September 1865, Governor William Marvin set the tone when on a stop in Jacksonville he warned residents:

> The spirit of malice and revenge must be banished from among us, and every one must embark in a mission of peace and good will. If you would see your fair land happy, inviting capital and good citizenship to come among you, you must see to it that Judge Lynch and his infernal cohorts are never allowed to scourge the country again. Let every one yield supreme obedience to the laws, and prosperity will follow.[2]

In the decades following the 1860s, Marvin's warning about mob violence and lynching proved prescient. Between 1876 and 1895 threats of mob violence periodically emerged as a direct result of the actions of law enforcement.

In April 1876, a black porter from the Windsor Hotel was admiring a campaign flag for the upcoming municipal elections at the railroad wharf. A black barber named Alex DeLyon, reportedly drunk, verbally accosted the man over his perceived support of the candidates. Officer Nolan noticed that his language became "boisterous, profane, and indecent." Nolan demanded he stop since "ladies" were disembarking the steamer *David Clark* nearby. When DeLyon refused, Nolan arrested him. DeLyon pulled out a straight razor and lunged at the officer who then pulled out his revolver and shot DeLyon in the chest. Nolan received a two-inch cut on his face from the razor. As DeLyon was sent to a doctor, a large crowd gathered around Nolan. The newspaper reported that black men on the wharf who witnessed the event surrounded Nolan, verbally abusing him and yelling "kill him!"

Sheriff's officers, including a black officer named Alonso Jones, arrived to help get Nolan off the wharf. The crowd grew and made Nolan's removal from the scene difficult. The mob then followed behind the omnibus that carried Nolan to the county jail where he was "technically arrested." The *Daily Florida Union* claimed that over two hundred black men and women surrounded the jail, calling out "kill him!" "break down the fence!" "burn the old jail!" Sheriff's officers guarded the space between the jail and the mob. Officer Robert Hearn, a black officer, was taken and beaten by the crowd. A white supporter of the sheriff was chased off by the mob. After an hour the *Daily Florida Union* reported that the crowd dispersed.

According to the paper there was some debate about the incident as to whether Nolan should have used a baton instead of a gun; however, prominent residents—black and white—spoke out against the mob and its actions. The newspaper took the position that the officer's actions were justified because his first responsibility was to the "preservation of the peace."[3] The "Wharf Mob" mobilized as a response to the actions of Officer Nolan and their perception that Nolan acted unjustly. Although the crowd engaged in limited action—just the bruising of Officer Hearn—their presence in the streets was theatre in the way a political rally or labor strike presents some grievance or call to action. To appease the crowd, the sheriff's office arrested Nolan, albeit just to quell the crowd and protect Nolan and the sheriff's office from the mob.

When police officer Carlton Lowe was shot on 26 February 1890, only the threat of a mob emerged. Lowe was called to a disturbance at a cigar store at the corner of Bay and Clay streets. According to witnesses, Lowe ordered Robert Armstrong, a black patron, out of the store for throwing a banana peel on the floor and verbally abusing the owner. Witnesses saw Armstrong ask Lowe his badge number—to which Lowe opened his coat to show his badge when suddenly Armstrong shot him in the chest killing Lowe. James Weldon Johnson recalled his mother telling him another version where Armstrong was walking along the street and dropped the banana peel on the ground and Officer Lowe ordered him to pick it up. When Armstrong refused, Lowe beat him savagely with his baton, and in the melee Armstrong grabbed Lowe's gun and shot him in the chest and killed him. This indicated that there was a counternarrative to the Armstrong story within the black community during this time. In fact Johnson was away at college during these years and recalled his mother being cryptic about the events in letters, but she provided the full story to him when he returned.[4]

Unlike the DeLyon fray, Armstrong was referred to as a "black brute" by the local paper, which reported him running through the streets crying "I lost my hat, but I killed the white son of a b——h." Armstrong was arrested the following day hiding in a swamp outside of town. When he arrived at the county jail, a large crowd had gathered, presumably white since their race was not mentioned. An African American woman the *Florida Times-Union* described as a "yellow creature" ran through the alleyway screaming "he ought to have done it! he ought to have done it!" The newspaper reported that when incidents like this occurred, it was not uncommon for black women to take to the streets in an "attempt to incite riot." Whites were reported to have considered the "wild and foolish talk of lynching," while blacks planned to mobilize and surround the jail to protect the prisoner from a lynch mob. The paper concluded that "the better class of colored people . . . deplored the murder and agreed that it should be avenged by due process of law." According to the paper no whites and blacks organized any mobs to address the murder of Lowe or the arrest of Armstrong.[5]

The "Wharf Mob" and the murder of Lowe would be dress rehearsals for what local whites referred to as the "Race Riot of 1892." On 4 July 1892, a fight between Frank Burrows and Benjamin Reed, co-workers at Anheuser-Busch Brewing Company resulted in Reed accidently killing Burrows. Reed showed up late after a delivery and Burrows reprimanded him, which was the catalyst for the altercation. Reed later claimed that Burrows called him a "black son of a bitch," to which he responded by punching Burrows. In the fight, Burrows fell on the concrete floor crushing his skull. He died hours later. The *Florida Times-Union* referred to Burrows as a "young white boy" who did not stand a chance against that "Giant" and "Goliath of a negro" Reed.[6]

News of the death traveled fast, and rumors of a lynch mob organizing soon emerged. Burrows's family lived in Mayport, a town in the northern part of the county, and a number of fishermen from there were reported to have been planning to take revenge. By eleven in the evening, black men with guns started to patrol the streets in front of the jail. The *Florida Times-Union* claimed that only the "riff-raff of the colored population" were out in the streets, while the "respectable" class knew "that the law in Duval County recognizes neither black nor white, but deals out equal justice." City officials wired the governor, who put the state militia on notice while the local militia camped at the armories throughout the night.[7] In the same way, the newspaper reported one narrative and blacks circulated a counternarrative. The newspaper referred to these actions as the forming of a "mob," but in hindsight this functioned more as a "countermob" to keep a lynch mob from forming.

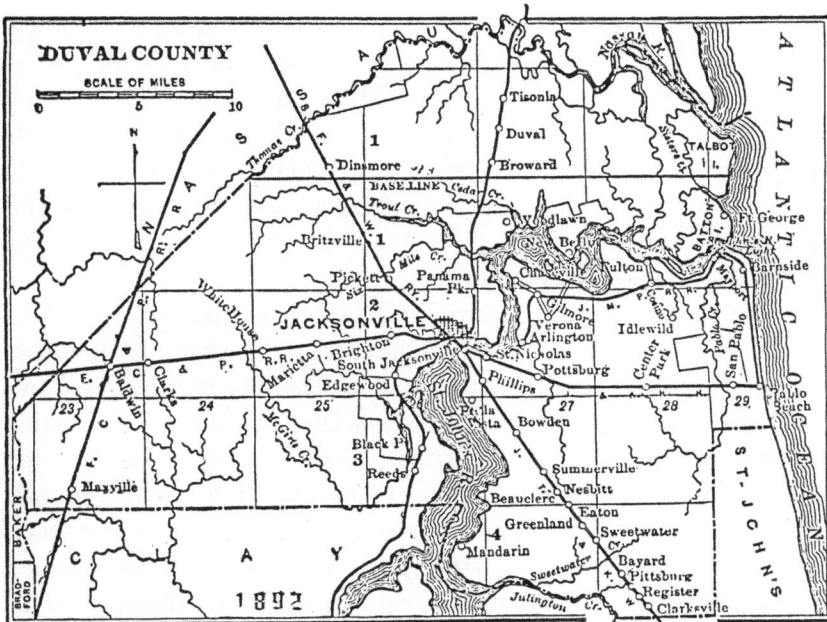

Figure 6. Map of Duval County, 1892. Jacksonville Public Library.

The execution of black mobilization throughout the three days of tensions was too organized and orderly to be spontaneous. Estimates of black men and women in the hundreds were said to be patrolling the streets armed on all of the blocks surrounding the jail and visible in the windows of the houses and apartments that surrounded it. The jail was in the predominantly black area of the city and therefore the surrounding dwellings were inhabited mostly by blacks. Newspaper reports said that blacks posted sentinels on the surrounding blocks who interrogated white pedestrians to determine their intentions for traveling within the vicinity of the jail. Black sentinels communicated through whistles, signals, and handshakes that white residents were proven to be no threat to the safety of Reed.

Numerous stories of members of the countermob harassing whites turned up in the newspaper coverage. Police Chief Paul G. Phillips stated he "circulated freely among the negroes who were there, finding everything quiet and no signs of any attempt at lynching." Even the *Florida Times-Union* stated that "the negro mob that gathered at the county jail Monday was amenable individually and collectively to the law." This was remarkable considering there were white men who taunted the counter-mob openly with threats of lynching Reed. The strategy on the part of the countermob was to not gather more than three persons in one place and to circulate around the streets and city blocks so as to not assemble in a group or crowd. They believed this would not make cause for an arrest, which according to Phillips did not raise any serious alarms for him since he did not arrest anyone during that time. This was not at all like the "Wharf Mob;" it was too organized.

At the end of the week, Alonso Jones, a former black officer for the police force who had been on duty at the onset of the wharf mob incident, was arrested as a ring leader, which would indicate that his experience and training informed the countermob leaders. James Weldon Johnson stated that this was part of a plan years in the making—more than likely hatched after the death of Officer Lowe in 1890. Johnson said Jones bought enough rifles and ammunition for every black family in town. Johnson also stated that a black cook named Dan Tresvan was arrested as well who claimed that his participation in the mob was predicated on his membership in a black secret society.[8] It would seem that the entire black community planned for this emergency with Jones providing the weapons and training and local black fraternal organizations providing the covert network to organize the action. Paul Ortiz catalogued numerous cases of black political organizing through fraternal organizations similar to this during this same time in Florida.[9] Emanuel Fortune Jr. probably first germinated this idea in an editorial for the New York Age. In 1889 he suggested:

> The law of self-preservation receive honor and use from the Caucasians, and when we note the fact that in nearly, if not all of the Southern States, colored men are murdered without cause, it behooves us to adhere and practice more than we do the first law of nature. Let us organize for mutual protection. Let us prepare in the present for the future. If we do this we will be helping to hasten the day when inhuman and cowardly murders of colored men in the South will be known no more.[10]

Fortune was responding to a Florida Metropolis editorial months earlier that advocated lynching in cases where the criminal justice system was too slow to act. While the Florida Times-Union publicly condemned lynching during this time, their reporters did not have a clear understanding of how the countermob was trained or organized and more than likely could not have conceived of blacks working secretly to subvert a lynching in the months or years leading up to the arrest of Reed.[11]

As with the murder of Lowe, the paper reported black women spread throughout the city whipping up the crowd and actively participating in the effort. Black women were said to be leaning out of windows with shotguns as well as carrying kerosene threatening to burn down the city in the event of a lynching. Additionally blacks came in from St. Augustine and Fernandina to augment the men and women patrolling the streets. On the afternoon of 6 July, militia companies from Gainesville, St. Augustine, and Daytona arrived by train to support the local militia who had recently taken to the streets. By midnight, most of the countermob had dispersed and were replaced by the militia units. The *Florida Times-Union* commended Sheriff Napoleon Broward who, with the support of the militia, arrested blacks who remained on the streets armed and still patrolling the blocks surrounding the jail. The paper claimed victory in that officials were "determined to have neither lynchings nor mobs here."[12]

Few incidents were reported. Thirteen black men who were armed and assembled at the corner of Bay and Liberty streets were arrested on the morning of 7 July. One police officer reported being fired upon that morning as well. The only victim was a member of the Metropolitan Light Infantry named Harry R. Stout who caught a bullet in his leg accidently fired by a rifle dropped by someone in the jail. The orderly conduct of the mob did not ally fears in local whites. The local branch of the United Confederate Veterans met at the Knights of Honor lodge and passed a resolution affirming that they "will be always ready to respond to any call for the preservation of good order." White men from Georgia also came by train who wanted to protect the city from "black desperadoes who threatened its very existence."[13]

As a result of the panic by local officials, Mayor Henry Robinson petitioned the Board of Police Commissioners to suspend Chief Phillips for not taking "precautions . . . to prevent the gathering of crowds and excited persons from coming to the vicinity of the jail and gathering there for the purpose of disturbing the peace." Robinson charged that Phillips allowed the city to be ruled by a mob. Phillips responded that he traveled through the crowds and felt there were no violations of laws to arrest anyone. He also claimed that he reported to Sheriff Broward as Reed was in the county, not city jail, and thus did not have a high profile in the events that transpired. Robinson and the police commission were not convinced, and they suspended Phillips.[14]

Roughly thirty black men and women were arrested on charges related to creating a disturbance, interfering with an officer, drunk and disorderly conduct, and other infractions. Most of them were prominent black men and women. Almost all were fined five to twenty-five dollars or had their charges dismissed in municipal court. Those that were arrested on weapons charges were then additionally handed over to county authorities. The most severe punishment was handed to Alonso Jones who was fined and ordered to serve ninety days in jail. He was bonded out and soon escaped to New York, where he lived the rest of his life. John E. Onley, William M. Artell, and J.B.L. Williams chaired a committee of black leaders and sent a resolution to the mayor that stated the justification for the counter-mob was because the city did not move quick enough to quell any threat of lynching and thus blacks felt it was up to them to act decisively. The committee further committed to "having every confidence in the fidelity of the colored citizens to the state and the county and city authorities." The Republican Club too passed a resolution denouncing "lynch law" and "requested" blacks refrain from any further mobilization in the future because it would provide "their enemies with political arguments to be used against them." The *Florida Times-Union* ran an editorial on 9 July that warned local blacks that white residents would not tolerate future mobilizations. The editor claimed that it was clear now that local whites were committed to thwarting lynchings, and the mob amounted to a rejection of white authority over the state's impartial prosecution and protections of all its citizens.[15]

As a countermob, it was successful in achieving its goal of stopping a potential lynching. Although thwarting a lynching was its primary purpose, a secondary consideration was the symbolism for what the mob stood for within the context of the role of black civil rights and the state. The countermob of 1892 was a critique of the lax nature of the Southern white criminal justice system and how little regard it had for black suspects. What happened to the tactic of the countermob after 1892 is unclear, but an editorial in the *Florida Times-Union* declared that the only way to stop lynching in the South was through a muscular defense of the jail, which would detract a lynch mob.[16] It is clear the idea of protecting a prisoner from lynching became conventional wisdom by this point. This action did not stay confined solely to Jacksonville. Countermobs emerged later in Key West and Dunnellon, Florida, to thwart lynchings, and Ida B. Wells mentioned the actions in Jacksonville as potential policy remedy to address lynching.[17]

On 8 April 1895, Police Officer Edward Minor was killed in a shoot-out with a murder suspect. This time the racial narrative was complicated by the fact that the suspect, Alexander "Kid Charley" Simms, was black and a gambler of questionable moral character. He not only killed a white police officer, he had also murdered Bud Stultz, a black leader well liked within the African American community. Additionally, Minor's brother, Lieutenant James Minor, headed the posse to apprehend Simms and frequently worked with and in this case hired black detectives in his ranks. These interracial networks created a much different response than the cases in 1890 and 1892.

The *Florida Times-Union* reported that soon after Simms was in custody, a small black mob formed around the jail. Rumors spread that white men were organizing to lynch Simms. To avoid a lynching, Police Chief Phillips put a decoy Simms on a buggy to catch the train headed for Fernandina, where a mob composed of both whites and blacks were lying in wait. Simms was taken south of the city to catch the train to St. Augustine. According to the *Times-Union,* both blacks and whites wanted to lynch Simms. The black mob at the train station and jail cried out to the officers present that they could take care of Simms by stringing him up.

The veracity of this story is hard to discern. The newspaper quotes the black mob as calling out "You turn dat man over to we niggers and we have him where the law won't find him. He will be a dead nigger in a half hour." It is hard to believe that two years earlier blacks in Jacksonville were able to pull off the 1892 countermob and then have such a sizable number of blacks reject the idea of protecting the life of the accused in 1895. Additionally, in newspaper accounts when blacks referred to themselves as "niggers" and the suspect as "nigger" seems more evidence of *Times-Union* propaganda than factual reporting. It is more likely that blacks did not listen to the threat from the 1892 countermob issued by local white city leaders and this was a similar effort albeit on a smaller scale. For the paper, possibly the easiest way to sell this story and not exacerbate further tensions would be to explain that the lynch mob was racially integrated and shared a singular purpose.

What makes the Simms case intriguing is the fact that the state, by way of the sheriff's office and police force, responded quickly to a potential lynching. With the actions of Lieutenant Minor involving black detectives and the plan to move the prisoner covertly to St. Augustine, black countermob leaders probably felt they did not have to respond the same way as in 1892. However, in 1901 the détente between local black leaders and law enforcement was again threatened. In November 1900, Police Officer Henry Raley was shot by the leader of a criminal gang that the *Florida Times-Union* called the Bridge Street Gang. A black mob was reported to have formed, but the newspaper indicated that it was an effort to free the suspect John Baxter, not to usher him into protective custody. Baxter made it to jail and was tried four months later in Bradford County and sentenced to life and hard labor for the killing of Raley.

Local law enforcement officers were visibly distraught over the verdict, taking to the streets and publicly crying that as "long as negro murderers are allowed to go unhung" the streets of the city would be unsafe for police and citizens alike. It would seem with this event the perception of punishment for black crimes against white law enforcement officers had changed, because not all blacks convicted of killing a police officer were executed up to that time. After several trials, in 1897 Robert Armstrong was determined to be insane and was paroled several years later. Clearly after 1901 for many whites it would not be the expectation that blacks who killed police officers could expect anything other than the death penalty.[18]

The trial and sentencing of Baxter marked an important shift in the attitude toward lynching and black criminality in the city. Editorials in the *Florida Times-Union* had begun to argue that a possible solution to thwart lynching was to be proactive toward black criminality. The editors recommended that the state make the "punishment of crimes more certain" and thus relieve the temptation for would-be lynchers.[19] Although conservative whites wished blacks would be less visible in the public sphere, blacks continued to organize and engage the public through a covert counterpublic. Sophisticated networks of black organizations and mobilization produced not only a discourse on black suspects in the criminal justice system but also pushed white leaders in local and state government to enact reforms.

5

Representations of Private Spaces

The move to push African Americans out of the public sphere had a direct impact on the ways in which private and public spaces were produced. Henri Lefebvre identified spaces that transmit the meaning of social relations and are tied to the "order" that imposes those social relations as "representations of space." Racial segregation was an example of "representations of space." Racially segregated spaces—whether public or private or through de facto or de jure means—was a way to embed white supremacy and the everyday practice of racial difference throughout Southern society. Not only did these spaces encode racial difference, but as David Harvey notes, these spaces were produced as a means to keep the subaltern or populations on the margins "in their place." As such, these spaces were also loci for not only contestation but also a publically engaged discourse on the segmentation of Southern society. Although white Southern politicians and policymakers conceived of Jim Crow segregation as a way to encode and enforce racial difference, it also brought a formal end to democratized space introduced by both Northern whites and blacks during Reconstruction.[1]

The attempt to segregate spaces can be divided into two categories: private and public spaces. Private spaces such as schools and churches began to racially segregate as a voluntary effort at the end of Reconstruction. As Howard N. Rabinowitz observed, while not an absolute, blacks in the South preferred churches of their own that would demonstrate autonomy from white control.[2] However, schools were different. As the state took interest in the private spaces of the classrooms, it pitted Northern missionaries against state lawmakers and brought an end to democratized private spaces throughout the city. It also pushed Northern whites and their descendants across the color line, eventually leaving black leaders and activists alone to address the political implications of Jim Crow on the limits of black citizenship.

The social construction of separate racial spaces that evolved into Jim Crow segregation would happen slowly over time. The first statewide attempt to legally reconstruct space after Reconstruction occurred with the passage of two pieces of legislation in the spring of 1881, which targeted the private spaces by making it illegal for blacks and whites to marry. In fact, it went so far as to legally define blackness as one-eighth black blood and carried much stiffer penalties to white men marrying black women to prohibit "black" children from inheriting historically white land and property. Additionally it punished white men who violated their mythic role as the paternal figures of blacks. The debate over interracial marriage would even be reinforced in the 1885 Florida Constitution. The ways in which this legislation was a means to cast blacks in racial and gender terms, as both less than whites and less than men, was not lost on blacks themselves. Thomas V. Gibbs decried that lawmakers gave license to white women to engage in sexual liaisons with black men outside of marriage, but only enforced these racial marital prohibitions exclusively toward black men.[3]

Locally, integrated schools and churches would not last long. Their evolution as racially segregated spaces was initially voluntary and not state mandated. In 1876, one Northern visitor wrote a letter to the *Florida Times-Union* describing several white tourists attending a fundraiser in the black suburb of La Villa for the opening of the local AME Church.[4] As integrated as this space was, it represented more an aberration in church attendance than a rule by this point in time. Additionally, since these white visitors were guests and not members of the church, their presence in a black church did not raise concern with local whites. In December 1875, Margaret E. Winslow a New York temperance activist and visitor to the city, noticed racially segregated churches by voluntary association. In a letter to *Zion's Herald and Wesleyan Journal*, she explained:

> There can be no mixing of the two races. The whites do not desire the presence of their colored brethren, and the negroes do not desire it. They prefer to take care of themselves, spiritually, socially and politically.[5]

However, according to Winslow, the color line in spiritual gatherings was sometimes fluid. In a subsequent letter she noticed that blacks and whites stood in the rain together for an hour in front of Metropolitan Hall to hear the northern evangelist speaker Dwight L. Moody, thus suggesting there was still some fluidity to the color line in public spaces.[6]

Yet early in the 1880s, several local pastors and church officials visiting the city witnessed separate churches for the exclusive use of either white or black parishioners without a return to the postwar integrated churches.[7] Thomas J. Abbott, a Northern Methodist pastor living in South Carolina, observed that with the large number of native-born Northerners, Jacksonville would soon be the "Boston of Florida." Yet that migration from the north did not deter the growing color line in church services. Upon a visit there in 1876 he stated:

> We have two churches in Jacksonville, divided. . . . we cannot say color of the skin, because there are as [many] white people in Zion's Methodist Episcopal Church as in Trinity . . . "because God has created of *one blood* all nations;" so we find difficulties whenever we attempt to divide, and the only safe and Christian course is to dwell together in love, as God designs, letting these characteristics take care of themselves, for naturally we all belong to Adam's race.[8]

Abbott, like the Northern missionaries that came with the end of the Civil War, clung to a racial egalitarianism predicated on Christian fellowship that was soon passing away.

Past associations and Christian camaraderie across the color line branded Northern Methodists as unsavory with the local white native-born population. A white Methodist pastor from Brooklyn, New York, named Adna Bradway Leonard, visiting the city in 1881, found it difficult

Table 5. Number of persons born in North in Duval County, 1880

Year	Born in Mass.	Born in Pa.	Born in N.Y.
1880	217	167	647

Source: Historical Census Browser. Retrieved 4 March 2012 from the University of Virginia Geospatial and Statistical Data Center, http://www.fisher.lib.virginia.edu /collections/stats/histcensus/index.html.

to reach out to local whites since the Northern Methodist churches had such close associations with the local African American Methodists. Leonard remarked that, "there are some that come . . . and cannot bear the reproach of belonging to a 'nigger Church,' and so they leave us and seek less reproachful associations."[9] Leonard's observations were taken as quite an attack by Samuel D. Paine, the pastor of Jacksonville's Trinity Methodist Episcopal Church. Paine thought that since Northern visitors and Northern-born residents only worshipped in his church, Leonard was accusing him of abandoning the more liberal ways of social engagement prevalent in the North. To defend his spiritual leadership, Paine confessed that the Florida Conference was mostly African American with only seven white men, and the lack of white support motivated at least one Northern Methodist pastor to leave the congregation and join the Methodist Episcopal South.[10]

This problem was even more compounded when at the 1883 Florida Conference, black and white church leaders agreed to formally split the "work" of the church along the color line, finally seceding to local impulses. Paine's final testament to succumbing to the pressure of respecting the color line appeared in 1888 when Bishop Willard F. Mallalieu eulogized Paine's tenure at Trinity by recognizing that even though he was a Union commander during the Civil War, "ex-Confederates sent in a most complimentary and earnest petition to have Dr. Paine continue in Jacksonville."[11] Both Leonard and Paine would agree that Jacksonville was not the Christian racial egalitarian community that Civil War era African Americans and Northern white missionaries hoped it could become.

While Northern Methodists could not maintain integrated churches after the Civil War era, they still constructed some semblance of racial integration within the private schools they oversaw, albeit without the racially egalitarian spirit of the earlier generation. As Reconstruction winded down, Northern missionaries opened new schools to prepare blacks for occupational and spiritual engagement on their own.

The Cookman Institute was probably the most well-known school privately educating African Americans. The school was founded in 1873 by members of the Trinity Methodist Episcopal Church with Samuel B. Darnell serving as pastor and principal during its first decades. The school was originally conceived around preparing black students for "manual labor" or industrial education, but soon promoted a curriculum of liberal arts education as well as some seminary preparation for black clergy.[12] By this time there were no public high schools—either black or white— so Darnell and the other founders hoped that Cookman would serve to prepare future black civic and spiritual leaders under white guidance and supervision until blacks could sustain such institutions on their own.

Also during this time, the Freedmen's Aid Society took over the Stanton Normal School, which originally opened as a public school for blacks after the war but passed between public and private hands throughout this time. In 1870, Stanton had one teacher reserved for white students, which suggests that although the school was racially integrated, students within the school were separated by race. During this time Stanton and Cookman took in white students, but only in nominal ways. Stanton in the late 1860s recorded only one white pupil and Cookman enrolled Darnell's daughter. Both Stanton and Cookman were integrated spaces with strictly drawn hierarchical spheres defined by race. Day-to-day operations, management, and instruction were left to whites, although some blacks did teach. Students, however, were almost exclusively African American.[13] At Cookman black men and women were trained in separate classrooms with separate curriculum. While black men had some exposure to the liberal arts, they too received some industrial education, and black women were schooled in "the duties of housekeeping, wife and mother." By the 1880s the Women's Home Missionary Society opened the Boylan Industrial Home for white women to train black women in the "home arts" and Christian worship. The Boylan classrooms were not exclusively black: in 1902 the Boylan Industrial Home reported serving Chinese and Syrian women who recently immigrated to the city.[14]

Although many white Northerners conceived of these schools as integrated spaces, there was a consensus among them that Northern educated white Christians would oversee and control that space, since to them,

Southern blacks were not ready to teach and preach equally alongside whites. On this point Winslow confided in the pages of *Zion's Herald and Wesleyan Journal:*

> The blacks, carrying their habits of idleness and want of responsibility into a state of freedom, have as yet amounted to very little, socially or industrially. A few earn good wages as waiters at hotels, and display their gold or silver watches upon every possible occasion, but the majority seem idle, and hang around street-corners and depots in rags and dirt; while the few in Florida at least, who have reached anything like respectability and competence are said to have been trained in slavery, and never to be of those who have come to maturity since emancipation.[15]

She further scolded "Northern Christians" for being too "supine" with their efforts to oversee black progress and commented that Southern whites were eager to again become the sole paternal figure in black Southern society. On one trip in 1881, a group of evangelical visitors from Cincinnati were shocked to find the Cookman Institute classrooms and chapel empty one Sunday morning, questioning the effectiveness of the "brethren" who oversaw the school.[16] Public school rooms were segregated along the color line down to separate schools for black and white children, and although the spaces in these private schools were racially integrated, administration and faculty positions were with few exceptions strictly defined by race.

The issue of black schools and black instructors did not end with Reconstruction. Even though John R. Scott's campaign to launch an AME Church supported school never materialized, some African Americans spoke about the desire to see black students, teachers, and administrators throughout the city have access to and opportunities for an education as prominently as whites. In 1885, Emanuel Fortune Jr. advocated that more black-run schools emerge because "it is not always the good fortune to find a man like Prof. Darnell who is wedded to the good work of elevating and educating the colored people of the South." By 1885 there was a white public high school and no black public high school, and the AME Church school was an attempt to try and rectify that imbalance. In a militant tone, Fortune advised blacks to "demand a high school or cause the one run for white pupils to be done away with."[17]

The specter of the freedman Jesse Brooks and the marriage to his former plantation mistress cast a long shadow over the black private schools. A social experiment fourteen miles to the southwest would capture the attention of the state and nation and finally bring an end to any integrated space in the schools in Jacksonville. In 1884 the American Missionary Association (AMA) opened a church in Orange Park, a suburb of Jacksonville populated mostly by migrants from the northeast. The AMA introduced the church for the spiritual patronage of both races; however, like the churches in Jacksonville, administrators reported to have only white members. As the community and church grew, parish members opened a private school with funding coming from wealthy evangelical Northern families. The Orange Park Normal and Industrial School opened in 1892 and offered industrial, home arts, and agricultural training without distinction to race. Unlike Cookman, Boylan, and Stanton, strict racial spheres of hierarchy were not as clearly defined in the space populated by students. The AMA made a great deal of the experiment in Orange Park and publicized its efforts throughout Northern magazines and church publications.[18]

The town of Orange Park was designed by its Northern migrants to be a place where public space could be redefined in contrast to the increasingly rigid control of public space in Jacksonville. Previously the site of the town was the location of the antebellum Mackintosh Plantation. In 1873 Harriet Beecher Stowe founded a school with some living quarters for local area African Americans that had since been abandoned. Although cotton plants in full bloom and sugar cane were the natural reminders of the property's previous tenure, the town founders took great care to remove the artificial monuments of slavery left by the previous owners of the land. They discarded the whipping post used to publicly punish disobedient bondsmen and women, and within "a gun-shot away" town leaders built the Orange Park School. In that place they cheerfully claimed that "the grandchildren of those who once danced and howled to the strokes of lash or paddle now learn the lessons of liberty and peace."[19]

Mary C. Jackson, a black reformer from Atlanta, visited the Orange Park School on several occasions upon the request of its principal Amos W. Farnham. In 1892 and 1893 she wrote articles about the social experiment taking place on the grounds, in the classrooms, and throughout the living quarters of the school. She witnessed white and black pupils learning and living side-by-side. She claimed that initially the white students separated themselves from the black students, but as the year went on the classroom and living spaces became comfortably integrated. All students were separated by gender, which was the policy in public and private education at the time. Jackson noticed, however, that the male students at the school formed closer personal bonds interracially than female students. Jackson concluded that the fault for this lay with the black girls, whom she believed harbored resentment toward white girls and women as social and occupational impediments to the economic mobility of educated black women. Throughout her yearlong visits she pointed to the coming problems for the long term viability of this experiment.[20]

For Jackson, there was no unified white support or tolerance from the Northern migrants. She claimed that

> a majority of whites in Orange Park are New Englanders, who have been there for some years. . . . It is a bitter pill, however, because many of them are *southernized* Northerners. At first they strongly objected, and more than once used their influence to have the colored pupils withdrawn, but with no effect.[21]

This rift was further exacerbated when in 1893 a black student applied and was granted membership to a white church, which resulted in a heated debate between members. Jackson noted that this action had then "gone outside the southernized New Englanders and has struck the real Southern spirit."[22]

Jackson's articles to the *Independent* about the Orange Park School give us a window into how black reformers and community leaders interpreted the redefining of public space during this time. In a response to Southern editorials, Jackson offered the idea that slavery arrested the Christian progress of both Southern whites and blacks:

> Their [Southern whites] barbarism did not consist in wigwam huts and tattoed [*sic*] skins, for they reveled in luxury, had churches and

schools; but the very foundation of their religion and education was antagonistic to those principles which characterize the highly civilized—morality, virtue, brotherhood of man and Fatherhood of God.[23]

The fact that so many Northern migrants agreed with Southern whites on segregation confounded and disillusioned Jackson, who conceded that Southern whites did have the virtue of openly displaying their bitterness toward blacks while Northern whites only did so privately behind closed doors.[24] For Jackson and other supporters of the school, integrated public space along the precepts of racial egalitarianism was the only true marker of freedom, constitutional equality, and humanistic Christian progress.

As any other American city during the time, Jacksonville and its surrounding communities such as Orange Park were not static population centers but places where the steady increase of residents was a permanent characteristic. This demographic reshuffling led the state superintendent of instruction, Albert J. Russell, to declare in 1890 a crisis due to the fact that so many African Americans were leaving the rural districts of the state for the "cities, towns and villages." This observation was reiterated by William N. Sheats, his successor, in 1894. By the 1890s the state noticed the capacity problems in black urban schools. To accommodate this migration trend, state officials claimed that new black schools emerged, both public and private, while the number of white schools stayed stagnant. Russell and Sheats defended their policies to their critics by stating that the state spent quantitatively less for black schools, but that funding was concentrated in a few urban areas while monies for white schools were spread throughout the entire state.[25] Sheats, however, did not stop to appease his critics with the financial details of school funding; soon into office, he made the strict separation of the races in private schools a critical initiative during his tenure. It took him a full year, but in the spring of 1895, Sheats successfully lobbied the state legislature to pass a law strictly enforcing racial segregation in all private schools, clubs, and fraternal societies.[26]

Winslow's prediction concerning native white Floridians reasserting their paternalistic role over black life would find no greater advocate during this time than Sheats. Sheats saw the experiment in Orange Park not only personally offensive, but also the perfect excuse to wrestle Northern influences from the Southern landscape. For Sheats the issue of who controlled space in the private schools was tied up in the state's economic dependency for Northern capital and investment. He admonished Northern critics by stating that

> The true Southerner is Anglo-Saxon and American in every fiber of his being and he will continue to combat all the blandishments of wealth and seductions of power, that his home and his schools may remain for all time the hot bed for germinating a sentiment that shall plead for social distinctions and the purest type of Anglo-Saxon and true American manhood.[27]

Sheats wanted to settle the issue of who ultimately controlled space in these private schools. "Northern influences" into race relations in the South was a question not only of race and masculinity, but also patriotism and colonialism. The contours of this debate were not lost on critics in the North. One editorial in the *Chicago Daily Inter Ocean* asserted that if the state would not allow Northern parents the right to select and patronize the schools of their choice then "northern men and their money shall remain in the north and leave the blighted condition of Florida to remain just as it is until the narrow minded and bigoted natives who legislate for the state alone to develop it their own way." The editorial also pointed out the inherent contradictions in Sheats's philosophies since white Northerners would have no quarrels with the state if they decided to put their children in "a lazaretto or house of prostitution" alongside black children.[28] Thus in cases of contagious diseases or sexual intimacy, the color line would not apply, but in education and social uplift it had to be rigidly enforced.

The Orange Park School, as well as Cookman, Stanton, and Boylan, were the front lines of Sheats's effort to confront Northern modernity in the form of industrial capitalism. He claimed that

> the blind greed for a dollar ... in [the North] ... fails to look forward to posterity, or even to acknowledge that it has any claims upon the present, but we of the South propose to teach it to our children and to hand it on down as a dutiful legacy from generation to generation to vigilantly protect their race purity and social order against the insidious encroachment of social equality cranks.[29]

According to Sheats, the long tradition of race relations stretching back to the Old South and more important the preservation of caste or racial distinctions would be obliterated by the "equalists" pushing social equality and economic modernization. Sheats pointed to the number of Northern interracial marriages and projected that if the economy and social manners of the North were allowed to spread to the South, with its higher proportion of black population, then the South would soon resemble the mixed-race societies such as Haiti, Mexico, and Jamaica. Thus Sheats wanted the "strong arm of the state" to protect young white boys and girls from what he perceived to be an impending social calamity.[30]

The importance of space codifying the social ordering of Southern society was not lost on people outside the state. J. Cleveland Hall, a pastor from Danville, Virginia, urged Northern critics of Sheats to understand that blacks in the South represented a lower order of the race because of their bonded and rural heritage, while blacks in the North were more socially elevated. Thus Hall admonished Northern liberal reformers who assumed that there was some social equivalency between Northern urban blacks and Southern urban blacks. Sheats, however, did not share this perceived nuance. Hall's point drew a sharp rebuff from George S. Dickerman, a Connecticut pastor who vacationed in Orange Park and Jacksonville during the winter months. Dickerman professed to have shared public and private space with blacks throughout Orange Park and Jacksonville. From this experience he concluded that there was no difference between Southern and Northern urban blacks and challenged Hall and Sheats to visit the school and surrounding community, neither of whom had ever done so.

It is quite telling to notice that Dickerman did not challenge the caste or class implications to the construction of space both Sheats and Hall emphatically professed. Instead Dickerman implied that the egalitarian sharing of racial space in the classroom did not leave blacks and whites with the impression of social equality but only mutual understanding. To Dickerman it was unnecessary to clothe racial caste distinctions in the construction of space, because those distinctions were obvious. The refrain that civil rights and equal justice should be meted out blindly before the law even though the "colored races" were inherently inferior to the white race could be heard as a chorus at the fiftieth anniversary celebration of the AMA in Boston in October 1896. Both Dickerman and the

AMA had turned the page on racial egalitarianism, which represented a growing trend within the ranks of Northern whites.[31]

As the 1895 fall school year opened, the Orange Park School's ambitions concerning its color-blind policies were drawn back significantly. According to the *American Missionary* magazine, school leaders claimed the impetus for white enrollment came from the parents who had no educational options for their children otherwise. The article further pointed to the fact that white students occupied "different rooms in the dormitories, different rows of seats in the chapel, and different tables in the dining hall." If true, this was a departure from what Jackson observed between 1892 and 1893 and possibly a precaution to conform to the "Sheats law" as it was commonly referred to in the Northern press.

Supporters of the school depicted themselves as innocent bystanders to Sheats's self-aggrandizement. They claimed that although students were not completely segregated in the classrooms, chapel, and dining halls, the school separated white and black students within those spaces to denote the racial differences the law intended to preserve. However, Northern ecclesiastical organizations, such as the National Council of the Congregational Churches of the United States, passed resolutions professing that the civil rights and Christian privileges of the Northern white teachers were being violated by the law and demanded the AMA take this fight to the U.S. Supreme Court if necessary to protect the rights of private institutions to teach without "distinction of caste."[32]

A game of chess followed between the Orange Park School and Sheats. Intent on breaking the law as a form of passive resistance and to test it constitutionality in the courts, the school officials opened the year with white teachers and black pupils living in the same dormitory building. Later on, the white teachers decided to dine in the same room with the black pupils. The anarchist newspaper *Liberty* concluded that Sheats ignored this and "jumped into the bramble bush and scratched out both his eyes." Undaunted, school officials gave the order by January 1896 for black and white pupils to again occupy the same classrooms. On 10 April 1896, the Clay County sheriff was charged with arresting the pastor, principal, five teachers, and two white parents of the Orange Park School. The *American Missionary* summarized this action as the state taking "the guardianship of manners and morals out of the hands of those who have planted and sustained the institutions until now."[33] As the state and Sheats believed that the social construction of space was to be controlled by whites, whites also in this case could only be held legally liable in violating the law. When the school was founded in 1892, it was not formally a black school until whites locally and statewide took umbrage. The very existence of blacks as patrons made the space, in the minds of many whites, an inherently black space that could not also be occupied equally by whites.

On 22 October the circuit court in Clay County declared the law unconstitutional on a technicality. All the officials, teachers, and parents of the Orange Park School were released because the judge believed the title of the law too vague. Although this decision fell short of validating Sheats, it was not perceived as a victory for the Orange Park School or the private black schools operating in Jacksonville. The following school year Augustus Field Beard, superintendent of the AMA schools, declared that greater care was taken in separating the races at Orange Park, and the AMA believed "that such commingling of the races as now exists in the South is thoroughly wicked."[34] The Cookman Institute in Jacksonville too conformed to the law during this time. The denouement of the state's intervention into private black schools occurred in 1913 when Sheats pushed through a policy banning teachers and pupils of different races within the same classroom. Administrators at the Cookman Institute claimed this was Sheats's attempt to remove white women from positions of authority in private black schools. For the white men and women working at Cookman and Boylan they mounted no resistance to this policy because they believed the courts would uphold the law. Some white women involved too expressed the fact that it was not worth spending time in jail next to criminals and libertines in order to fight this unjust measure, so they decided to quietly recede into the night once and for all.[35]

The process by which private spaces—such as churches and schools—became rigidly racially segregated also demonstrated that blacks no longer had allies in Northern whites to maintain democratized spaces. Even though the descendants and remnants of the white Northern racial egalitarians reluctantly toed the line on racial segregation by the twentieth century, racial segregation was by no means settled. Churches and schoolrooms were spaces that were somewhat static, and although fires, renovation, and new construction could change their appearance, what was a space for prayer or education in 1865 was conceptually the same in 1913. Thus customs and laws governing that space could have a continuous application. However, public space on transportation could not be as well defined throughout this period due to travel between separate civic jurisdictions, the introduction of new technology, and new systems of transportation. It would be the production of racial space on public transportation that would provide another outlet for the black public sphere.

6

Representations of Public Spaces

The racial segregation of churches and schools followed a linear path from a state of flux, where racial space was ill-defined, ultimately to a point where the state and local governments stepped in to rigidly define space in the private spaces of the classrooms. Laws to reconstruct racial space on public transportation were not as amenable over time as new technologies created spaces that were introduced to the public landscape for the first time. Although the social construction of racial space in churches and classrooms did not test black activists' philosophies toward social egalitarianism, their fight against Jim Crow transportation would. Unlike churches and classrooms, spaces on public transportation had to be shared due to the costs of incorporating separate cars for the exclusive use of two races. Those fixed spaces had to be separated for joint use—and as such it pitted blacks and whites interracially and intraracially over the meaning and production of "equal" space. In this environment the contestation over space on common carriers pushed black activists to organizing within the black counterpublic to combat and negotiate the production of racialized spaces.

The South lagged behind the North and West in transportation technology and infrastructure. This introduced unique problems for the production of public space on railroads after the Civil War. One Northern traveler to Jacksonville in 1873 observed

> that many of the refinements in railroading which obtain in other parts are but little regarded here and a system of practical simplification prevails. We have an example of this on this "Florida Railroad," for we found that the distinctions of trains as "express," "mail," "accommodation" and "freight," are quite unknown. Our train combined all these, having, behind half a dozen freight cars, two for passenger—one each for whites and colored citizens; who notwithstanding the Civil Rights Bill . . . persist in riding in separate carriages.[1]

The fact that Florida railroad accommodations offered much less space than those in other regions would be a point of contention for railroad employees as well as black and white passengers alike.

The most famous case to bring attention to the issue of racial public space on Florida's railroads was the ejection of Daniel Alexander Payne, senior bishop of the AME Church. He was traveling on the Florida Central Railroad between Jacksonville and Fernandina when a conductor removed him for refusing to take a seat in the black or "smoking" car. At this time there was not an established racial seating policy on railroads servicing the state, but white working-class conductors assumed the role as sole arbitrators of public space on the cars. This absolute authority was not always recognized. Before Payne in August 1881, J. W. Killgaard, another conductor on the same railroad, was arrested for "compelling a colored man to ride in the second instead of the first-class coach."[2]

The calculations he took to plan his travel really spoke to the anxiety and frustrations more privileged blacks faced maneuvering around racial discrimination on public transportation after the Civil War and before de jure segregation. Payne spoke of his preparations for the trip, and due to the fact that he was frequently asked to move from the white first-class car during railroad travel, he decided to exclusively travel by steamer since he did not have "difficulty" on a boat. Being an older system of public transportation, steamer travel was longer and more infrequent, but according to Payne, by taking a steamer he could avoid "railroads and all other public carriers . . . [where] the heathenish and barbarous color regulation prevails."[3]

Before Payne booked his steamer travel, he was assured there would be no "difficulties" by the local ticket agent. Payne purchased a first-class ticket for a train that had only two passenger cars, one "reserved" for blacks and white consumers of tobacco commonly called the "smoker," and the second car reserved for first-class white customers. One observer noticed the differences between these two cars in the following way:

> [T]here are coaches labeled, "For White Passengers," which are comfortable, having matting on the floor, parcel racks, gas lights, decent vessels filled with fresh drinking water, and other accommodations while the cars marked "For Colored Passengers" are filthy, badly heated, and poorly lighted, often without water, and always full of tobacco smoke and spittle . . . which a respectable Northern railroad company would not have on their tracks, even for scavenger purposes.[4]

Payne walked to the back of the first-class car before he was stopped by Samuel B. Darnell the white pastor and president of the Cookman Institute. Darnell asked Payne to sit next to him to chat about a recent ecclesiastical debate illuminated in the Methodist newspaper the *Christian Advocate*. Payne claimed that he was heading to the black car; however, when Darnell requested his company, Payne assumed this granted him permission to sit next to a white passenger. This exchange either went unnoticed or ignored by William E. Livingston, the white working-class conductor, who promptly informed Payne he needed to relocate to the black car or get off the train.[5]

When faced with this "difficulty" Payne was originally trying to avoid, he demanded the train stop immediately so he could walk back to the station. Passengers were reported to have yelled "shame! shame! shame!" in a show of support for the aged bishop. Upon exiting the train, Payne later recalled turning to Livingston and saying,

> I have traveled over many portions of foreign lands, and found no such treatment. I also came from Baltimore to Jacksonville having no trouble, and I want to know if white men riding between Jacksonville and Fernandina are better than white men elsewhere.[6]

These incidents between black passengers and white conductors touched on the interclass animosities between affluent blacks and working-class whites in the production of space on public transportation. One supporter of Payne speculated that only lowly white men would be conductors on the railroads because "gentlemen" would never stoop to enforce the racial policies of the company. Payne claimed that as the train pulled away from him he heard Livingston yell, "Old man, you can get on behind, if you choose." An offer he took as an insult, and one which he claimed to reply with "contemptuous silence."[7]

What the Payne incident demonstrates is the ambiguity surrounding the proscription of racial space on public transportation during this time. Since Florida railroads had less passenger cars than other parts of the country, there were no "ladies" cars for the exclusive use of privileged white women. The first-class car doubled as a "ladies" car, so white men who wanted to smoke or chew and spit tobacco entered the "smoking" car, which on Payne's trip doubled as the "black" car. Unlike his traveling companions, Payne inquired and purchased a first-class ticket, presumably to sit in the first-class car; yet he was conscious of the fact that his intention was not to sit next to or fraternize with whites, until he was requested to do so. The owners, operators, and agents of the railroad company all allowed Payne and other blacks like him to maneuver through these ambiguous spaces because of his reputation and privileged background. However, the white working-class conductor refused to recognize these exceptions and policed the racial space on the cars with a strict adherence to making the first-class car less inclusive of blacks and conversely allowing the "black" car to be more inclusive to whites.[8]

After complaints from white and black supporters of Payne, the railroad manager apologized and guaranteed him travel on the railroad in the first-class car on a later trip or on any after.[9] Support also came from an unlikely place in Judge Joseph Wofford Tucker of Sanford, Florida. Tucker had been a secessionist and Confederate boat runner, but moved to Sanford after the war and became active in the United Methodist Church. Tucker wrote a public letter of rebuke in the *Florida Daily Times* stating:

> I do express profound regret that Bishop Payne should have been ejected from the cars for any reason excepting such as depends on deportment and payment of dues. A man who had character enough and talent enough to preside with grace and dignity over the

Methodist Ecumenical Council in London, when called to do so, as one of a list [of] eminent men who took part as chairman in such a presidency; a man who had learning enough to submit a written dissertation for the instruction of that body; a man whose moral character is unspotted, and who has devoted a long life to the Lord Jesus, was, in my humble judgment, good enough to ride in any car on that railway. . . . All right-minded Southern people will contemplate the matter with pain and regret.[10]

Tucker's letter must have struck a chord with native white Southerners, because he soon fired off a second letter to the *Daily Times* speculating that Payne's demeanor provoked the altercation and affirmed that "[t]he federal courts have adjudicated the right of corporations to make this discretion for public lines of transportation." Tucker suggested that Payne was treated humanely in this encounter and thus should not feel insulted or abused. Payne's reply to this was "[i]f a man be bound with silken cords and then sold as a slave, he is none the less a slave than if he were bound with chains of iron."[11]

Black civil rights activists in New York and Baltimore mobilized to protest the Payne incident and held rallies and sermons in those cities denouncing the Florida railroads. Both protests demanded that the New York and Maryland legislatures pass laws recognizing the rights of African Americans to travel equally with whites on public transportation. In New York at a rally at the Bethel AME Church, activists passed a resolution demanding blacks throughout the South willingly violate these railroad policies and sit in sections reserved exclusively for whites. There was a great deal of pressure on Payne to take this case to the courts and follow it as high as the U.S. Supreme Court. In one editorial the *Christian Recorder* urged him to "[p]ursue the wrong doers even to the Supreme Court of the United States, and bring down upon them the heavy hand of the General Government."[12] He refused because he believed that the American court system was blinded by racial prejudice, which was a prescient action since the following year the U.S. Supreme Court handed down their decision in the 1883 Civil Rights Cases declaring that Congress and the federal government had no authority to enforce the Fourteenth Amendment on private businesses and institutions.[13]

The ensuing protest touched on the class implications of Jim Crow. Payne and other activists demanded that railroad companies provide a first-class black car, as other Southern railroad companies. The men organized religious leaders in Jacksonville, across the country, and called upon Methodist leaders in England to condemn the fact that they, as esteemed men of the church, were subjected to the lowest moral character of the white race. They complained that as church members and pillars of their community they must remain quiet and content to sit alongside poor whites they believed frequented brothels and contributed to an atmosphere of low moral standards within the "smoking" cars.[14] They did not take offense to poor blacks whose behavior might also offend them, because these activists were the self-professed leaders of their race and had an obligation and duty to chastise and reform the moral character of poor blacks. However, poor whites who committed the same offenses in the cars left them powerless as respectable men and women of color, thus denying they embodied gentlemanly manhood and respectability as social elites.

Payne and others involved in this protest believed that this fluid practice of segregation was an attack on their own manhood and their collective journey as a race of people toward civilization. If they challenged or tried to reform the moral character of poor whites, white society would perceive this action as an open challenge to white supremacy or worse, proof of social equality. Allowing this race-mixing in the black cars was a constant reminder to privileged blacks that they were socially unequal no matter their upbringing or perceived respectability. Their solution was to maintain rigid racial segregation so poor whites and privileged blacks would not compete for authority within the same public space. One report suggested that black newspapers around the country demanded and raised money for a legal defense to ensure "separate cars for colored and white passengers, and [so] no whites were allowed to ride in the colored car, which was as comfortably furnished as that for the whites."[15]

Their message also targeted the social hypocrisy of the train companies' policies. As Tera W. Hunter points out, after the Civil War, whites acted to fit blacks into roles of subservience to whites instead of independence from them.[16] Black activists noticed that railroad officials allowed black nurses and servants to sit in the first-class car with their employers, a practiced allowed by law before the war for slave owners and bonded servants while traveling. Payne and other activists believed that whites were rewarding blacks that embodied the symbols of subservience. They believed that whites were comfortable with blacks who reinforced their own nostalgia for slavery, and black leaders as the respectable and intelligent class of blacks were more offensive to racist whites. Since respectable blacks could not integrate white space on public transportation and demonstrate to white America that they achieved refinement and civilization, they instead sought to remove less-privileged blacks from white space so visages of black social inferiority would not be so accessible to whites.

Payne and these activists thought that the only way African American society could prosper was to allow for the natural black aristocracy to emerge and lead the race by example. As Kevin K. Gaines has demonstrated, black abolitionists used the language of the Enlightenment to claim that slavery disrupted and corrupted not only the natural rights, but also the natural order of African American civilization.[17] To Payne, an abolitionist educated in the North, this idea was not foreign. Payne believed railroad policy circumvented this natural social evolution, placing poor blacks in spaces reserved for white privilege and placing poor whites in positions of social authority over the black aristocracy. Their solution was to maintain a rigid color line so that black leadership would emerge autonomous from all white influence and replace the white political and social leadership they believed controlled black society during slavery and Reconstruction. The leaders of this movement demanded that blacks boycott trains that had a segregation policy and did not provide rigidly separate and "equal" accommodations.[18] They hoped this economic tactic would create a more equitable system that was consistent and judicious when separating the races.

Other privileged blacks did not rely on boycotts to protest the racial policies of the trains; they went through the courts. When Alice Williams, a black woman, entered the first-class car on the Jacksonville, Tampa, and Key West Railroad in September 1886, the conductor and brakeman forced her into the "smoking" car. Williams claimed that since she was "decently and becomingly dressed, and behaving in a modest, decent and lady-like manner" she deserved to sit in the first-class car.[19]Similar to the Payne incident, the conductor physically intervened to enforce railroad policy. Like Payne, Williams believed her respectability afforded her a degree of privilege on the train that could not be recognized by traveling in the "smoking" or "colored" car.

Williams appealed to Victorian era notions of womanhood and sexuality to claim that the white conductor viciously attacked her. She argued that, beyond the embarrassment of being dragged face down by her legs to the "smoking car," she also suffered permanent injury to her body. This injury threatened her womanhood in two ways. First according to her testimony, she was so battered and bruised she could not maintain the housekeeping that not only threatened her womanly duties but also removed her from her occupational sphere. Second, and more important, she confessed, the confrontation caused inflammation to her womb, which kept her from both conceiving children and from sexual intimacy with her husband—a duty that fulfilled her womanly role in affirming her husband's manhood and sexual dominance in their relationship, the bedrock of Victorian era sexual values. Thus from this incident Williams claimed that Jim Crow threatened her as a woman. From her description of the incident, it is clear Williams appealed to the notion that Jim Crow segregation, specifically the enforcement of it at the hands of working-class white men, would upend the Victorian social order between men and women and the privileged and the poor.[20]

The legislature, mindful that the state had a stake in maintaining an image as a land of peace and tranquility for Northern travelers, believed that a policy of racial segregation would decrease the number of inter-racial conflicts on the railroads as experienced by Payne and Williams. The legislature passed a law requiring that all railroad companies provide separate accommodations. A committee of black leaders from Jacksonville sent word to the governor approving of the legislation as long as the railroads and government enforced equal with the same vigor they enforced separate. Caesar Andrew Anthony, a black New Yorker who spent time in Jacksonville, commented that "some system should be devised by which people who pay full price for tickets may be protected from association with the vulgar and vile if their own color and the abandonment of the other."[21]

Lawmakers eventually incorporated the egalitarian language that black leaders demanded, demonstrating that black leaders were part of the legislative process to define segregation. The law specifically stated:

> [A]ll railroad companies doing business in this State shall sell to all respectable persons of color first-class tickets, on application, at the same rate that white persons are charged: and shall furnish and set apart for the use of persons of color who purchased such first-class tickets a car or cars in each passenger train as may be necessary to convey passenger equally as good, and provided with the same

facilities for comfort, as shall or may be provided for white persons using and traveling as passengers on first-class tickets.[22]

For black activists this was only one component to ensuring equality of public space on common carriers. The law directed conductors to ensure that whites could not "ride, sit, travel, or to do any act or thing, to insult or annoy any person of color." The conductor could be fined for not enforcing racial segregation against whites the same way against blacks.[23] Building upon this measure, the state legislature in 1891 passed a law clothing all train conductors with police powers while in passenger spaces in order to maintain order against unruly, intoxicated, or vulgar patrons. The law went so far as to deputize passengers as "willing" agents of order to assist the conductors. Although maintaining segregation was not specifically mentioned as a category to preserve "order," the implications of this legislation would have a chilling effect on relations between affluent blacks and working-class white conductors on trains.[24]

The optimism black leaders held out for the enforcement of "equal," however, soon passed once they learned that not all railroads supported the spirit of the legislation as they had envisioned it. Still, after the measure had been in place for some time, cases came before the Florida courts in an effort to negotiate some semblance of "equal" accommodations.[25] By the late nineteenth century the fight over civil rights in regard to public accommodations was really one of defining "equal." Black leaders referred to unequal accommodations as Jim Crow cars because they were meant to not only separate, but humiliate, black passengers.[26] Blacks hoped they could help create a system that separated the races, but did not become Jim Crow.

Some black leaders abandoned any legislative or judicial measures to alleviate racial discrimination on the railroads. Thomas V. Gibbs found hope only in the economic gains of blacks as a whole. In response to the railroad legislation he stated:

I am candidly of the opinion that the solution to the race problem is wrapped up in our material progress. As the one unfolds the other will appear. When our people as a mass learn to ride the railway cars without eating water melons, fat meat, and peanuts, throwing the rinds on the floor; when our women leave their snuff sticks, greasy bundles and uncouth manners at home, railroad discrimination will abate much of their injustice.[27]

According to Gibbs, the actions of the black masses kept respectable blacks from social uplift in the minds of many whites—demonstrating that the issue of racial segregation probably did not create a uniformity of opinion between affluent and working-class blacks.

The issue of racial segregation on public transportation moved from the railroad to the streetcars soon after the end of the nineteenth century. In Florida, the push for segregated streetcars hit Jacksonville first. After the Great Fire of 1901, racial tension increased in Jacksonville due to the migration of poor blacks and whites attracted to labor opportunities in rebuilding the city. Throughout the summer of 1901 local papers reported racial incidents and confrontations on the city's streetcars. One June evening, shots from an unknown origin killed a young black boy riding a streetcar, which then caused riots on many of the lines.[28] Similar to the cases involving interracial conflict on trains, the city council introduced a bill to segregate the races on the streetcars as a measure to quell any future conflict.

A streetcar segregation ordinance became law in November 1901 in the face of opposition by two black and two white city councilmen who represented opposite extremes of the issue. The two black city councilmen rejected any ordinance to separate the races, especially one that put police powers in the hands of the conductors. The two white city councilmen objected to the ordinance because they did not believe it went far enough in separating the races.[29]

Black activists and church leaders mobilized quickly to defeat this measure. They formed a committee to lobby Mayor Duncan U. Fletcher not to sign the bill, placing blame for the tensions squarely on the backs of poor blacks, specifically the migrants who had arrived in the city since the fire. Black leaders pleaded with the city council and mayor that the "Home Negroes" were not to blame for the tensions on the streetcars. Instead they suggested that the poor "ignorant" class of blacks sat next to whites on the streetcars and refused to acknowledge the customs and traditions of sitting apart from whites; whereas local blacks or "Home Negroes" understood and appreciated this custom.

Reverend Elias J. Gregg, pastor of Mt. Zion AME Church, admitted that the black migrant element were particularly "obnoxious." He appealed to the mayor's Southern white sensibilities by claiming that respectable blacks opposed social equality; however, those same respectable blacks did not want to be subordinate to poor whites who regularly leveled indignities at all blacks on the streetcars. In fact, Gregg stated, by clothing white conductors with police powers to enforce segregation, the ordinance would only embolden poor racist whites to confront the respectable class of blacks even more. Other blacks on the committee re-iterated these same sentiments. They proposed that the mayor veto the or-dinance and instead construct more streetcar lines and create more space as a way to alleviate racial tensions.[30]

After the mayor indicated he would sign the bill, the committee and other black activists gathered at St. Paul's AME Church. Local doctors, lawyers, politicians, and pastors all spoke in opposition to the segrega-tion law. James Johnson, a local minister, demanded that they organize a boycott of the streetcar lines in protest.[31] In support of the plan, leaders of the local Hack Union agreed to lower rates for black customers to offset the cost and convenience of riding the streetcars. The committee agreed to pursue the boycott and lobby the mayor and streetcar manager to in-tervene. The resolution adopted at the meeting spoke out against white conductors and demanded all blacks refrain from riding the streetcars. According to the resolution, the leaders of the boycott believed that poor whites who worked as conductors would use their police powers solely to humiliate blacks—thus turning segregation into Jim Crow. They also appealed to the white business class and pointed out that blacks should not boycott and protest those businesses they felt had dealt judiciously with blacks to encourage privileged whites to pressure the city council and mayor to seek an alternative.[32]

Whites reacted in different ways to the protest. The mayor did acknowl-edge working-class whites had a tendency to treat blacks poorly; however, he believed that boycott leaders exaggerated their fears. Mayor Fletcher revised the language of the bill to include what he perceived to be more egalitarian wording, but black leaders still found it unacceptable.[33] Other whites welcomed the boycott because they did not want blacks riding the cars at all. In an editorial in the *Metropolis,* a white observer claimed that the boycott was the best thing to happen to the city in a long time:

That our colored citizens have imbibed some grains of sense with the whisky they indulge in is clearly perceptible in a resolution they ad-opted. . . . A new source of danger, however, arises from the pigeon-toed and bandy-legged pedestrianism which will ensue upon pave-ments, diminishing their qualities of resistance . . . and sidewalks of a more durable character will by some inventive genius be brought to the front. We accept the boycott proposition with pleasure.[34]

The author's views most likely represented those of the city's working-class whites. While the mayor and many in the business community were willing to engage and listen to black leaders and their concerns, this author clearly perceived blacks as one racialized group without any class distinctions. To the author all blacks embodied inferior moral and physical features of poor working-class blacks. To the leaders of the protest, this was the image and perception they were fighting to overcome; if all whites accepted this notion as representative of all blacks, it would empower the white working class.

Although boycott leaders spoke about a protest environment of cooperation between poor and privileged blacks, that spirit disintegrated within a week of the protest. On the night of 10 November, passengers on several lines heard shots fired at streetcars from unknown origins. Fearing attacks, conductors stopped all service and called the police to restore order. Some witnesses claimed blacks openly attacked conductors, in some cases firing bullets into the cars. Newspapers also reported that crowds of blacks targeted African American passengers caught riding on the streetcars. Although no one was hurt, black leaders quickly blamed working-class blacks for the violence and demanded the city move to end the segregation ordinance. They also pleaded with those involved in the riots to follow nonviolent forms of protest.[35]

It is hard to judge how popular this boycott was with less privileged blacks or even which segments of the community emphatically supported the boycott. News of the boycott appeared in many black newspapers outside the state. A black Cleveland newspaper claimed that women were central to the success of the protest. According to the reporter, women were the ones who took the lead on organizing the boycott. The paper claimed that women not only "boycotted" the streetcars, but also their husbands and lovers by withholding sexual intimacy from those tempted to ride. J. D. Howard, a black reporter from Indianapolis, implied that the violence on the streetcars was actually retaliation against those blacks who ignored the boycott and rode the streetcars. He claimed that most blacks in the city supported the protest and those who did not would do so under extreme risk because the "darkies were out for blood."[36] Ironically, Howard appropriated this racial epitaph as a tongue in cheek way

Figure 7. Photo of black-owned North Jacksonville Line, 1902. George Baldwin Papers, Southern Historical Collection at the Wilson Library, University of North Carolina at Chapel Hill.

to describe what he believed to be the racial solidarity and singularity of mind of the participants even though this movement was really about getting whites in the city to recognize black class distinctions.

By the end of November, black leaders organized a new phase of the protest. They decided to create a transportation company to service the black neighborhoods of the city. Local leaders launched the North Jacksonville Line, which was black owned and operated. They advertised this economic venture as part of the formal protest of segregated policies on public transportation. Black newspapers wrote stories about this venture and encouraged their readers to invest.

During its first year of operation, the company employed only African American conductors and managers. The company also sought to address some of the questions of equality that nagged them about segregation on the white-owned streetcars. On the North Jacksonville Line, the white section of the car was in the back and the black section was in the front reversing the space of Jim Crow. Since it also serviced the poor white working class sections, this was a way to respond to the class issues central to black leaders.[37] By this time, newspapers stopped reporting the protest and the streetcar managers reported that blacks were again riding the streetcars.[38]

While the boycott and ordinance left the front pages of the newspapers, they remained part of the negotiations between white conductors and black patrons. In 1902 the Stone and Webster Company, a Boston-based utility conglomerate, bought up most of the streetcar lines in Jacksonville. George Johnson Baldwin was manager of the company's Southeast corporations. Located in Savannah, Baldwin maintained close communication with the Jacksonville branch. There he hired Judson Douglas Wetmore, a black lawyer and city counselor to work for him secretly, inform him of any potential protest from black activists, and then work with him to undermine it. In Jacksonville, either through the advice of Wetmore or as a measure to help encourage black patrons, Baldwin's company instructed all conductors to adhere to the segregation ordinance by being quiet and courteous and not enforcing segregation emphatically.[39]

During this time, segregation on Jacksonville streetcars still did not require a separate section, only that conductors instruct people of similar racial background to sit next to each other on the same seat. However, even this milder segregation policy created problems because blacks, specifically black women, frequently tested the enforcement of these policies, as black women enjoyed a freedom of confrontation that did not engender the same response as that of black men.[40]

Two confrontations in December 1904 and January 1905 demonstrate that black women did not fear the consequences of confronting white streetcar conductors. A black woman with her aged father boarded a car, each sitting separately. When the conductor asked the man to sit with his daughter, she stood up and yelled to her father not to move, then pointed out to the conductor that her father paid the same price as any white person and deserved to be treated just the same. According to the report, the women became verbally abusive to employees operating the car. White passengers then threw her off the car. The streetcar manager reported to Baldwin that this was the second black woman that day removed from a car after being asked to sit with other blacks. Weeks later, two daughters of a prominent minister boarded a streetcar, one described as "negro" and the other described as "mulatto"—both "well dressed." The "mulatto" sister sat next to a white woman and the woman did not object, so the conductor did not approach her. As the car filled, some whites were left standing. The conductor asked the "mulatto" sister to move to the seat next to her "negro" sister so a white passenger could sit down. The "negro" sister became abusive not only verbally, but physically as well, scratching the face of the conductor. The foreman boarded the car and asked the "negro" sister to move next to the "mulatto" sister who then yelled, "she shan't move, she shan't move." The foreman summoned the police who forcibly removed both women from the car. Their father, one "Reverend Brown," soon thereafter called a meeting noting that the streetcar company was now enforcing the ordinance with vigor and wanted to organize some course of action.[41]

White passengers, also, openly contested the enforcement of the segregation policies. As noted, white passengers and bystanders frequently took it upon themselves to remove "troublesome" black patrons. In Jacksonville, many white passengers demanded to know exactly what the seating policies were on the cars before they entered them. Often times the conductors would respond that there were no seating policies, which would enrage them further.

These types of incidents forced Baldwin to make sure that the conductors understood exactly what the policies were and how delicate conductors needed to be when enforcing them. Baldwin instructed his conductors to simply mention to patrons where they should sit. If conflict resulted, they were to walk away because they had done their job according to a strict interpretation of the ordinance.[42]

By the summer of 1905, the issue of racial segregation moved from streetcars to municipal elections. In Jacksonville, the challenger in the mayor's race made the issue of segregation on the streetcars his central focus. Major Wiley Toomer tried to discredit the incumbent mayor, George Nolan, by claiming that he did not enforce the segregation ordinance. Toomer suggested that Nolan gave a tacit override to the streetcar companies to ignore the ordinance. The incumbent mayor responded that he was waiting for the state legislature to pass a tougher segregation law before he acted. Nolan eventually won reelection; however, the issue stuck around the rest of the year.[43]

That spring, state legislators from Pensacola, Representative John Campbell Avery and Senator William Alexander Blount, introduced a statewide streetcar segregation bill that would eventually be known as the Avery Law. Avery was a well-known reform politician in the grassroots populist mold; however, Blount was a lawyer for Florida railroad companies and famously tied to corporate interests throughout the state. The bill and unlikely political alliance emanated from the imbroglio between the pro- and antimunicipal ownership forces from their home district. With a great deal of support from politicians and many whites in both Jacksonville and Tampa, not to mention the newspapers in Pensacola,

Tampa, Jacksonville, and Miami, the bill passed within a few weeks.[44] Since Blount spearheaded this bill in the state senate, it was another reminder to black leaders that ultimately "sympathetic" privileged whites would not stand up to segregation on their behalf.

Opposition to the measure came from black leaders in Jacksonville and Pensacola, who sent committees to lobby against its passage, and from state politicians from rural districts. Similar to Jacksonville years earlier, black leaders claimed that homegrown blacks knew to keep away from whites on the streetcars, and the migratory working-class element were the root of the problem. Similar to 1901, they suggested issuing more franchises and running more cars to alleviate the problem an unlikely solution in Pensacola and Jacksonville because it would have strengthened the position of the local streetcar companies where municipal ownership was most popular. The bill created tension between rural and urban forces in the legislature, and legislators representing rural districts had to be convinced to support this measure. One editorial in the *Pensacola Journal* recommended that rural politicians be taken on a junket to a city and to ride on a streetcar next to one of these "cullud" passengers, so they could understand firsthand the necessity of this bill.[45]

By this time, Baldwin believed this law was not worth fighting against and instead hoped to reform it. He hired Tampa lawyer and lobbyist, Peter O. Knight, who went to Tallahassee and met privately with Blount and Avery to amend the law to the liking of Baldwin. Knight believed that he could stop the law; however, the movement to pass this type of legislation was too influential to kill indefinitely. He hoped to help pass a weakened version of the law in order to avoid a stronger one passing in the future. Knight agreed to shape the law as close to the Jacksonville ordinance as possible. There were some aspects of the law Knight could not stop, such as conductors with police powers and separate compartments. At the last minute in the Senate, Blount added a provision to allow black nurses and servants to ride in the white sections if accompanied by their employers.[46] To the joy of supporters in Jacksonville, Tampa, and Pensacola, the law passed and Baldwin immediately had to address the potential of another lengthy and costly boycott.

Baldwin relied on a suggestion from Wetmore to help solve the problem of the state segregation law. Wetmore recommended that Baldwin follow the example of the streetcar lines of Atlanta, Augusta, and Macon.

Figure 8. Political cartoon from 1904 of J. Douglas Wetmore from the *Sun*. Wetmore passed for white periodically during his adult life. Here, he is depicted as a "dark savage." State of Florida Archives, Florida Photographic Collection.

In those cities streetcars had two entrances, one in front for white customers and one in the rear for black customers. Wetmore believed this was the long-term solution to the problem that would create a sense of "fairness" to the seating policy. Both Wetmore and Baldwin agreed that dual entrances would reduce the race tension and could curb any impending boycott.

Baldwin's streetcar line soon followed Wetmore's recommendations. Facing legal action from the city attorney, Baldwin refused to hang the signs and place the partitions separating the races until he was certain that the signs would not antagonize the boycott leaders even more.[47] Although Baldwin tried to compromise concerning the application of the law, it did not prevent another boycott. A group of black ministers, lawyers, and politicians in Jacksonville, Tampa, and Pensacola, organized boycotts independent of each other in response to the state law. Now Wetmore's services and confidence became more indispensable to Baldwin—a fact he boastfully acknowledged in many reports to Baldwin. Baldwin, too, became a target of whites, a *Pensacola Journal* editorial accused him and the streetcar company of being "nigger[s] in the woodpile." Supporters of racial segregation claimed that Baldwin truly was on the side of blacks and secretly supported and financed the efforts of Wetmore.[48]

The organized boycotts of 1905 were much different in spirit than the previous protests. Earlier, the leaders of the boycott concerned themselves with the impact of these policies on the respectable class, specifically those they referred to as "Home Negroes." The Inter-denominational Ministers' Meeting passed a petition supporting the 1905 Jacksonville boycott that declared that this law insulted all "Negroes." Protest literature and sermons from this group no longer suggested that black migrants somehow caused this tension; they continued however, to place blame on the white working class who served as conductors and motormen. It now appeared that conductors and motormen were no longer simply insensitive to privileged African Americans, but were abusive and created strife for all members of the race.[49]

One leader of the second Jacksonville boycott movement, Reverend J. Milton Waldron, pastor of the Bethel Baptist Institutional Church and chair of the Inter-denominational Ministers' Meeting, gave speeches at neighboring churches urging African Americans to stop riding the white streetcars. He energized his supporters by telling the story of a racist white conductor who pushed his daughter out of a streetcar. He claimed his daughter sustained an injury and died a few months later as a direct result of the incident. To stop future incidents such as that, he begged that protesters needed to attack the racist law that led up to such a confrontation. According to Wetmore, Waldron exaggerated the incident and used it to provoke greater support for the boycott. Wetmore claimed that his daughter died nine months after the incident of an unrelated illness, while the *New York Age* reported the death as directly related to the action of the conductor. Whether the incident led to her death or not was not as important as Waldron's use of the incident to evoke concerns for racial solitary. He informed the crowd that what precipitated his daughter's attack and subsequent death was racism. Some of the middle-class leaders of this boycott abandoned their goal for class acknowledgment and united many in the community under an umbrella of racial solidarity.[50]

It was Wetmore who devised a plan to help lessen the impact of the boycott. He reported to Baldwin that the group led by Waldron did not have support from all the black ministers within the city. In fact he stated that some encouraged their flock to ride the streetcars in spite of the boycott. Wetmore convinced Baldwin to publicly donate money and land to restore a local black college and churches located on the streetcar line, hoping this would be taken as a goodwill gesture by the black community and thus promote business for the company in spite of the protest. More important, he convinced Baldwin to finance a legal attack against the Avery Law led by him and a black Pensacola attorney named Isaac L. Purcell. Wetmore claimed that he found a loophole making the state law unconstitutional. Wetmore believed he could stop the boycott or at least slow it down by diverting attention from it.[51]

Wetmore failed twice to get a case through the courts, until a black man named Andrew Patterson sat in the white section of the North Jacksonville Line. Once the courts accepted the case, Wetmore tried to solicit funds from readers in black newspapers throughout the country to help his legal defense. His financial support actually came directly from Baldwin. Wetmore became a hero in local as well as national black newspapers for his fight against discrimination. How widespread support was for Wetmore or the boycotts in general one cannot tell. The *Pensacola Journal* claimed that only the bon ton class of blacks supported this protest, and poor and working-class blacks were indifferent to these racial policies. The *New York Age* reported that similar to 1901, some blacks in Jacksonville were patrolling the streets and intimidating would-be black passengers from riding the streetcars.[52]

Wetmore and Purcell questioned the Avery Law's constitutionality, but did so grounded in late nineteenth century sensibilities and notions of class and respectability. The two men claimed that since the law gave permission for African American nurses and servants to ride in the white section with their employers, it violated the Fourteenth Amendment and the Florida Constitution by not providing equal citizenship rights to all black Floridians. Wetmore and Purcell also maintained that the law made a special class of citizens out of both black nurses and white conductors. They argued that hypothetically the law discriminated against whites because African Americans who employed white nurses could not have their servants sit in the black segregated sections with them. The local circuit court found in favor of only one of Wetmore's arguments. The circuit and later the Florida Supreme Court judges admitted that although there would never be conditions under which African Americans would employ white servants, the law discriminated against whites because theoretically white servants could not enter the black segregated cars with their employers. Ironically, the law could openly discriminate against blacks; however, since this specific law discriminated against whites in theory— the Florida Supreme Court upheld it as unconstitutional.[53]

A closer look at the wording of Wetmore's arguments suggests that he adopted the same rationale as the 1901 boycott and the nineteenth century transportation protests. Wetmore wrote, "[the law] encouraged the servant class of [black] people and discouraged the more progressive and intelligent class."[54] According to his letters and the arguments against the Avery Law, Wetmore saw it as a protest to defend the respectable class against Jim Crow, a position that conflicted with Waldron and his direction for the protest.[55]

By November 1905, Jacksonville passed a municipal segregation ordinance that did not include any exceptions to the law for servants and nurses. As the *New York Age* noted, it would take only a minor revision to the Avery Law to get a Jim Crow law passed that would not be defeated constitutionally. The pessimism of the *New York Age* reached fruition in 1907 when the state passed a streetcar segregation law that allowed for servants and nurses to ride in the compartment of the race of their employers, and made no specific mention to it applying to any specific race of people. Wetmore himself mounted two more legal actions in vain. However, his last effort did not challenge the segregation law directly but the enforcement of the law as it applied to Patterson in 1905. In an interesting turn, the last high profile segregation case against a transportation company in Florida during this time involved a plaintiff named George Geiger who sued the Florida East Coast Railroad in 1913, not for forcing him to sit in the "Negro" car but for the conductor roughly pushing him to the car and subsequently pushing him off the train as Geiger protested his treatment. These two cases show that the legal arguments after 1906 did not attack the racial segregation policies but instead contested how these policies were enforced—a position that suggested the legal attack had no other avenue for redress in the courts.[56]

After his legal fights failed, Wetmore again suggested that the streetcar company employ the policies of Atlanta, Augusta, and Macon and install two entrances. He recommended that company representatives promote this action at the black churches.[57] The compromise ended the boycott in Jacksonville. As the grip of Jim Crow tightened, the city's two most prominent black leaders left the state. Months after negotiating an end to the 1905 protest, Wetmore moved to New York, never to return to live in Florida again, eventually marrying a white Southern woman there and passing for white until his death in 1930. His nemesis, Waldron, took over the Shiloh Baptist Church of Washington, D.C., in 1906, joined the Niagara Movement and the National Association for the Advancement of Colored People (NAACP), and died in D.C. in 1931.[58]

Even though both Wetmore and Waldron left Jacksonville, the political repercussions of the boycotts and legal challenges would have a great impact on black Jacksonville. By early 1907, conservative whites in the city decided to remove black representation from municipal government altogether. Ion L. Farris campaigned in 1906 for the state legislature on a promise to introduce a bill to redraw the ward districts so that the remaining two black councilmen would lose their seats in the 1907 election and thus create a greater political consensus on the council. This effort was a reaction to the 1905 streetcar fight, which cumulated in the gerrymandering of the black majority sixth ward with two bordering white majority wards. Local officials placed three hundred white voters in the sixth ward and secretly moved the voting stations in all white neighborhoods, thus adding an extra burden to black voters.[59] The two incumbent black city councilmen were defeated by white candidates. The following day in the *Metropolis* an editorial stated:

> The Metropolis congratulated the people of Jacksonville upon having selected for the first time in many years a full white City Council. . . . There is no real argument to advance why a minority party should seek in a city government a minority position as it has always been demonstrated here that the colored citizen received fair treatment from the white citizens. . . . the juries in our courts . . . are composed of white men and no one can say that these jurors ever rendered a verdict detrimental to any one on account of color.[60]

Although whites in Jacksonville believed the state and judicial system was "color blind," local blacks knew from their own experience that the

Figure 9. Political cartoon of 1907, gerrymandering of the Sixth Ward. *Metropolis,* 18 June 1907.

state and courts were blinded by color. Because of the gerrymandering of the sixth ward in 1907, African Americans in the city would no longer elect their own officials again until the 1960s.[61]

Unlike churches and schools, the production of public space on public transportation could not be autonomous space under the direction and maintenance of blacks themselves. Racial space on public transportation would always be contested space, and even after local and state legislation could be applied later to jitneys, busses, and taxis, black activists continued to protest and resist this racial space.[62] The movement to resist racial space on public transportation pushed black civil rights activists toward a rhetoric and organizing that was racially inclusive to blacks of different social backgrounds and proved that the black counterpublic could organize and speak to the mass of African Americans. Yet the fight over the construction of public space on transportation proved to blacks that working-class whites would be arbitrators of racial space on public transportation and would socially construct that space as spheres of racial inequality to cast all blacks as one inferior social caste.

7

Labor's Counterpublic

The black counterpublic was not the only one to emerge during this time. In Mary P. Ryan's *Civic Wars*, she tracks workers and white women who entered into the public sphere for the first time in the nineteenth century.[1] Similar to many other places, labor and woman suffrage counterpublics were organized with and without the inclusion of blacks respectively. Although blacks were indispensable to the creation of labor's counterpublic, black women were excluded from the woman's suffrage movement organized by middle-class white women. In many cases, since white workers and women were on the margins of the public sphere themselves, blacks were pushed even further to the margin within those counterpublics. Ironically enough, it was black labor in the saw mills who helped usher in the local labor movement and what would eventually become labor's counterpublic. Unions, strikes, and collective organizing were important to cultivate a discourse in the public concerning working hours and the right of labor to organize. As with other forays into public life, public space and how it is produced was central to the success of the movement.

When Jacksonville transitioned from a small agricultural community to an industrial seaport town, its workforce too transformed. Black
workers en masse moved to the city—drawn there with the availability
of skilled and unskilled wage labor. Like other industrial and port cities,
working-class residents soon took to collective organizing to protest for
higher wages and standardized working hours. Similarly to cities in the
northeast, public space would be the theatre by which workers collectively
voiced their grievances on display for citizens and civic leaders alike to
either witness or intervene. Maintaining a presence and often times policing public spaces afforded labor unions a chance to recruit and replicate
themselves. Black workers would always have a place in the local labor
movement; however, similar to the public sphere, they were pushed out
to the margins and ultimately had to form a black labor counterpublic to
engage labor's public.[2]

In May 1873 black lumber-mill workers organized a union they called
the Labor League. Throughout the numerous mills workers were exclusively black, and albeit short-lived, the Labor League represented not only
the first black union but also the first documented case of labor organizing in the city's history. A number of black mill workers organized the
union in private spaces and passed a series of resolutions to present to the
mill owners. Included in those resolutions were demands for more pay
and a standard ten-hour workday. At this meeting a number of men were
elected to take those demands to the mill owners and speak on behalf
of workers supporting the union effort. Their demands represented an
engagement with the public sphere where the union effort was under attacked by the dominant public. *The Tallahassee Weekly* lamented that, "the
mill owners will no doubt receive the committee kindly, but capital will be
able to hold its own in this country for many days yet. And shall we say
that it ought to be otherwise?" A reporter for the *Jacksonville Republican*
claimed that the union men believed that they were, "confidently trusting
in the generosity, and sense of right and justice of their employers."[3]

On the morning of 10 June, when the mill owners made it clear they
were not going to consider the Labor League's demands, most black workers in the lumber mills refused to show up. "Strike at the Saw Mills" informed the readers of the newspaper what happened to the negotiations.
The Labor League picked a curious time to go on strike because two of
the saw mills were undergoing repairs and maintenance thus employed
no staff. Additionally this was the summer that began the Panic of 1873,

Figure 10. Lumber mill 1870. Kellogg Album, Jacksonville Historical Society Photographic Collection.

so there was a surplus of men out of work nearby who were desperate enough to cross the picket lines.[4]

Although the strikers were flexible to the pay issue, their demand for a standard ten-hour workday was nonnegotiable. They claimed they were required to work up to twelve hours a day. Mill owners stated that in the summer months they required eleven- to twelve-hour workdays, but during the winter, workers worked no more than eight and a half hours. Additionally mill owners calculated breaks for lunch and changing of the blades when for at least an hour workers were not working. Intransigence from both sides continued throughout the strike.[5]

The action of the strike played out in the public space in and around the eight mills. At times this public discourse could get violent. A handful of men who did not support the union continued to work at the Alsop and Clark Mill. Mill owners claimed that threats of violence went out to their employees who refused to join the strike. At the Wallace Mill, a crowd of strikers reportedly threw bricks at workers not honoring the strike, which then quickly descended into more violence. The papers reported a striker named Valentine fired his gun at one of the workers not supporting the protest. According to the paper the police soon quelled the mob but not before Valentine and his target escaped.

Most of the mills closed during the three days of the strike. The Alsop and Clark and Penniman mills remained open employing white labor, reportedly from the rural areas outside the city. The Fairchild Mill opened with a skeleton workforce that refused to join the strike. By the fourth day of the strike, the local newspapers claimed that the protest collapsed and the leaders moved on to other cities. The papers also reported that many of the union members returned to work at their previous pay and conditions. All of which the *Jacksonville Union* believed was "more commendable than to hang out at the streets in idleness." In the way the strike was a public drama played for local citizens and officials, the workers' "idleness" afterwards too created a public spectacle that did not go unnoticed.[6]

Violence, however, did not remain isolated to the striking public space outside the workplace. The police arrested several men for breaking into the home of a nonunion mill worker named Barclay. During the trial, the prosecution claimed these men threw bricks at Barclay's house shattering his windows to intimidate him and his family, thus demonstrating that this labor counterpublic injected itself into the private spaces of the workers' homes. The paper reported that the defense offered no rebuttal or witnesses, and the mostly black jury erroneously returned a verdict of not guilty implying that the jury's verdict was a message of racial solidarity in the face of clear evidence of guilt. This demonstrates that the public drama of the strike swayed some segments of the local population. Since records of this event are scant, it is hard to know whether and if workers situated race within the context of this political discourse and thus the jury's actions reflected a broader racial solidarity or if the jury sided with the men as workers exercising a workplace grievance.

The dominant public challenged these actions and message. These sentiments did not work to convince the editors of the local papers. When a rumor circulated that Jacksonville native and sitting governor Ossian B. Hart might have met with the striking union leaders, a local paper said they hoped the story was not true because "it would be lowering the dignity of his exalted position."[7] With the context of the specific message aside, this strike functioned through the counterpublic of black workers who were able to communicate a political discourse that the jury understood and the local press felt they had to publicly deride in no uncertain terms.

Andrew Herod informs us that the purpose of a labor geography for the union movement is partly to replicate itself. Although a public or counterpublic is situated in a geography, the function too of a labor counterpublic is to replicate and promote the ideas of labor leaders and organizers. Out of the ashes of this unsuccessful strike and the Labor League, black workers formed the Colored Workingmen's Association, which was an unskilled labor union. Many chapters emerged in the northeast during this time by white workers to collectively demand more pay and an eight-hour workday across different artisan occupations. By 1886 the Jacksonville Colored Workingmen's Association joined with white mechanics to form the Florida Mechanic's and Workingmen's Association, which was a white skilled and black unskilled labor union. There were seven chapters throughout the city divided by race, but as city leaders would soon learn, they would come to work together through a counterpublic.[8]

In May 1880, a Connecticut printer named Elwood S. Ela visited Jacksonville and was horrified by the conditions of the saw mills. He said he believed he "stumbled across a corner of Hades." Jacksonville grew since the Civil War, and the mills around the bluff overlooking the port expanded to meet the thriving demand for lumber. Ela not only alluded to the mills as hell, but to him the black workers were figuratively the demons presumably working for the mill owners or through his allusion the gods of the underworld. Ela remarked how the mills, the port, and the trains operated day and night to meet the demand for lumber. It is certain Ela's literary hyperbolae gripped readers of *Zion's Herald and Wesleyan Journal*. To Ela, the mill owners, workers, and consumers were all one and the same in this industrial process, which debased and dehumanized the natural and unique environment surrounding the city.[9] For black workers, the thought of this process being a dehumanizing experience was not entirely lost on themselves.

During the summer of 1880 black mill workers again went on strike exclusively to standardize the ten-hour workday. This time around, the mill owners were not united in addressing these demands. The owners of the Alligator Mills conceded to the ten-hour workday, while the Alsop and Clark and Eagle mills offered an increase in pay instead of a ten-hour workday. The St. Johns Mill hired replacement workers and refused to negotiate with the strikers. On 23 June black mill-hands organized a general strike at all the mills where management refused the "Ten Hour System."[10]

Unlike 1873, this time around violence emerged in several places. On the night of 25 June at the Alsop and Clark Mill, a black police officer named Joe Nelson was mortally wounded by striker Benjamin Bird. The police were sent out to protect the nonstriking laborers who continued to work in the face of the protest. Several police and strikers were wounded that evening as well as the next morning when violence resumed. As a result of the melee, a citizens committee composed of prominent white and black civic leaders formed to meet with the strike organizers to negotiate a settlement, while the state militia met at the armory in preparation for martial law to be called.[11]

The strike leaders confessed to the committee that they had planned no violence at the protest and only wished to address their concerns to the workers who returned to the mill. They claimed that "the police were the aggressors and that they (the strikers) had at no time intended to break the public peace and create a disturbance." Colonel J. J. Daniel, former commander of the local militia and a representative from the committee, then informed the strike leaders the committee's objective was not to guarantee the right of labor to strike but instead sought "the preservation of the public peace." Gilbert Hunter, owner of the Eagle Mills, offered to pay extra for any hours worked over ten hours as a compromise. The strike leaders originally rejected this proposal but John Nattiel and Joseph E. Lee offered Hunter's proposal to all the striking workers again. The strike leaders eventually caved in and accepted the committee's proposal.[12]

Most of the striking workers ended their protest, but a small group refused to accept the agreement and continued striking publicly for another day until they gave up. One newspaper warned, "[t]here is still some dissatisfaction among the strikers, but hopes are entertained that there will be no further breach of the peace." One aspect of this strike that struck a nerve with locals, white and black, was the role that some white labor organizers played in helping to incite and organize the black workers. By 1880 white skilled and black unskilled labor reached across racial and occupational barriers to cooperate, and this strike was probably the result of those efforts. Not only did white civic leaders take umbrage at the thought of this type of interracial cooperation, but Joseph E. Lee, the black Reconstruction era judge, spoke indignantly about the possibility of whites leading blacks to organizing and violence.[13]

The *Fernandina Mirror* called for these white labor leaders to be tried and sent to work as convict laborers in the local turpentine camps. The *Florida Times-Union* went so far as to call these men "Kearneyites," which symbolized the political implications of these public actions. Kearneyism was a term used to describe the followers of San Francisco labor leader

Denis Kearney. Kearney was often criticized by opponents as a communist who used mass mobilization of white workers to attack union leaders, Republicans, and Democrats alike in rhetorical flourishes steeped in populism and nativism. His followers were said to be involved in many of the riots against Chinese laborers in Northern California, and his detractors accused him of using labor strikes and violence to confront and intimidate local political leaders. In kind, the *Times-Union* suggested these white labor leaders were manipulating the black strikers to create public discord for some political means as Kearney did in California. Alternatively, black and white civic leaders refused to believe that blacks would organize on their own as in 1873 or that there could be genuine interracial organizing. Interracial organizing cannot be dismissed so easily, since some time after this strike white skilled and black unskilled laborers formed a union albeit racially segregated.[14]

What the 1873 and 1880 mill strikes also demonstrated was the ways in which black strikers used public space to draw in mill owners and local civic leaders to address their cause. More so in the 1880 strike since it was bigger, more violent, and the city more populated than in 1873. Local city officials, the police, and the state militia felt compelled to insert themselves into this labor dispute for the good of the "public peace," thus demonstrating that this strike became part of a discourse in the public sphere. To deal with labor outbursts such as this, the city reconvened the Jacksonville Light Infantry, which was the local militia unit disbanded after the Civil War.[15]

Following the 1880 Mill Strike, the local labor movement grew as more unions formed to represent skilled and unskilled labor. Although unskilled laborers such as saw mill workers never again staged a strike, craft unions periodically went on strike. The most significant of which that involved black workers was the carpenter's strike of 1902.

On 18 July 1902 the recently formed Carpenter's District Council called a strike when the Builder's Exchange refused to accept an eight-hour workday and a twenty-five cent per hour standard wage. Locals 605, 627, and 224 went out against the Builder's Exchange with 1,050 men walking off the job, including union workers in the building trades who were not carpenters or joiners, and joining the protest in solidarity. The strike was also different from previous strikes because it was organized through the Central Labor Council, which included all local American Federation of Labor (AFL) affiliated unions, and this was the first time that black and

Figure 11. Portrait group of African American Carpenters Union, Jacksonville, Fla., 1899. American Negro exhibit, Paris Exposition of 1900, Library of Congress.

white unions protested together. Like the earlier incarnation of the Florida Mechanic's and Workingmen's Association, the local branches of the United Brotherhood of Carpenters and Joiners were segregated by race, making the Local 224 an all-black organization. Although the unions were separate, black and white locals often came together for meetings, festivals, and even "smokers" in a racially mixed setting.[16]

Carpenters in other Florida cities had recently been successful in securing the eight-hour workday for the building trades. Union carpenters in Key West earned the eight-hour day for all work on federal contracts in October 1900, while union carpenters in St. Augustine and Tampa earned the right to an eight-hour workday in their respective cities by May 1902.[17] The Carpenters Union in Jacksonville was next.

The strikes of the late nineteenth century created the framework by which striking carpenters brought attention to their demands and engage the public sphere. On the first evening of the strike, in front of the Labor Temple on Laura Street, the Central Labor Union and national AFL representatives held a rally and gave fiery speeches supporting the eight-hour workday and threatening local leaders that more unions would join the general strike to expand it beyond the building trades. The local newspaper the *Metropolis* mildly supported the strike by observing that "[t]he situation will prove unfortunate for the city if there is not an early adjustment of the present difficulties."[18]

Although union leaders pleaded with striking carpenters on the night of the 18th to "conduct themselves in an orderly manner" and refrain from engaging in any activities that could be "construed as a violation of the law," public interpersonal intimidation emerged in public places as a tool to limit nonunion workers as strike breakers. Similar to earlier strikes, violence and intimidation were employed as part of a broader labor public. To address workers who held out and refused to join the union, the local carpenters union targeted them as outsiders. Union leaders reported that they would be "getting along fine, but would do much better if it wasn't for the scums, scalawags and farmers flocking in here," presumably from outside the city. Sometimes union strikers confronted nonunion workers interpersonally. On the first night of the strike the police were called out to what they were told was a large-scale disturbance on Bridge Street, and when they arrived found only two white carpenters—one union and the other nonunion—verbally abusing each other. The Chief of Police William D. Vinzant informed the paper that he was beefing up the police presence. The next night the *Metropolis* reported that a mob of striking carpenters gathered at the corner of Cedar and Duval streets to persuade nonunion workers to join the strike. As the nonunion workers refused, the newspaper indicated the crowd got angrier and even threatened the workers refusing to join the strike. Eventually the police were called out to disperse the striking workers, who by then the police claimed had promised to do damage to the building and steal the tools of the nonunion workers. The tone and threats of the conversation as reported by the police were denied by the union. Union leaders believed this to be effective because they claimed to "have . . . succeeded in forcing the saw and hatchet men to go back to their farms or seek other fields, and no doubt we shall have the eight-hour day and better pay very soon."[19]

After one month the union started to see results. The Central Labor Union claimed that a majority of contractors agreed to their demands, and they were able to convince local merchants who signed a petition of support. The Central Labor Union also threatened a citywide general strike with bartenders, railroad clerks, washwomen, as well as other unionized workers joining the building trades. On 23 July the Central Labor Council called another rally in front of Laura Street with the newspaper reporting hundreds of workers showing up. The rally was called to demonstrate that the strikers were resolved in their position.[20]

In a newspaper interview, an official from the Central Labor Council stated:

> We are hopeful of success and if the people of Jacksonville will keep hands off we will show them the prettiest fight they ever witnessed. . . . On two or three occasions, men who are opposing the labor unions in this fight had made efforts to create a riot and thus endeavor to change the favorable sentiment we have won by our orderly conduct. . . . Only a few outside workingmen have come to the city since the strike, and we believe we will be able to prevent "scabs" from taking the places of the men. We are using all honorable means to this end.[21]

According to union leaders the public space was a theatre where labor leaders could plead their case to citizens and business and civic leaders alike and engage the public sphere. Opponents to the striking workers were cognizant of this and produced a counternarrative in the public space to dissuade support for the strike.

Although labor leaders frowned upon violence, they did acknowledge that violence was part of a greater discourse concerning the rights of workers and to some extent the rights of manhood. Robert L. Harper, an official with the Central Labor Council issued a threat to strike opponents who tried to introduce a counternarrative in the public sphere by violent means. He stated that the "men who are opposing labor unions . . . had made efforts to create a riot . . . to change the favorable sentiment we have won by our orderly conduct." He cautioned that, "Our men are law abiding, but they are men nonetheless and will stand up for their rights and those . . . attempting to create trouble will get their hands full if they do not desist."[22] The gendered interplay between strikers and opponents were fixed around notions of manhood and masculinity. Harper stated that strikers would maintain order in the ranks, unless their manhood was threatened, which could only be addressed through spontaneous acts of violence—all of which Harper claimed trumped a reasonable expectation to maintain order.[23]

The day after the public rally, the city witnessed a parade through downtown of roughly one thousand union workers—all carrying signs demanding the eight-hour day, which the newspapers described as peaceful.

The following day the *Metropolis* reported that "the song of the hammer" could again be heard throughout the city when a number of contractors agreed to the eight-hour workday, and union carpenters went back to work with them. In the days and weeks that followed more contractors joined their ranks with only a handful still holding out.[24]

The epilogue to the strike occurred on 5 August 1902, when workers changed the time in which "Big Jim" sounded the end of the workday. Big Jim was the steam whistle at the waterworks. Each day it blew at five o'clock in the evening to signal the end of the workday. But union leaders convinced the Board of Bond Trustees to switch the time to four o'clock instead to coincide with the eight-hour workday they claimed they won in the strike. Contractors who were still holding out protested to the board and claimed that a minority of workers in the city worked an eight-hour day and since a majority worked a nine-hour day the board should revert back to the five o'clock whistle. The board investigated and claimed that they could not come to a determination as to whether the workday ended at four or five o' clock and decided to leave the change in place. Thus when Big Jim blew for one and all in the public places in Jacksonville each day, he celebrated the victory of the carpenters' union.[25]

It took thirty years for a single trade to standardize the workday. Throughout that time what started as a movement by black unskilled laborers evolved into a craft protest of a racially segregated movement for the eight-hour workday. Each strike and each protest learned the lessons of how public space could be a theatre of action to involve the local population and civic and business leaders and bring their demands to the public sphere. Although the carpenter's strike seemed like the accumulation of a spark first ignited by black mill-workers decades earlier, it also represented the apex of interracial cooperation and coordination. After 1902 the local union movement pushed black workers to the margins.

During the 1912 streetcar strike, a racial fissure emerged between black and white unions. Like the carpenter's strike of 1902, the streetcar strike gripped the city over the question of the right for streetcar workers to unionize. The strike lasted a few weeks in the fall of 1912, and race became an issue during negotiations. George Baldwin, the Southeast manager for the streetcar company, publicly questioned if he granted the streetcar workers union recognition, then they would have to provide the same rights to black workers and could open the door to equal wages for black and white workers and thus threaten the color line.[26]

William E. Terry, Southern Organizer for the AFL replied that the streetcar union only represented white labor, and he merely wanted white labor to have the right to choose their own unions and protect their own interests. He stated that the union did not represent black labor, nor was black labor an issue in the negotiations. Terry believed the race issue was a negotiating tactic, and once everything was settled, the managers and business owners would never pay black workers the same wage as white workers. Thus the union would not be forced to represent black workers. Clearly, what Baldwin tried to do was to suggest that if the union succeeded, then the benefits of being white—like hirer pay and shorter hours—would be in jeopardy. During the third week of the strike a majority of representatives from all of the unions voted to join the streetcar workers in a sympathy strike. Although Baldwin's argument did not influence Terry or other strike leaders, Terry's response as well as the racial exclusivity of the movement was probably the reason black unions voted against a sympathy strike. There had been a number of exclusively white labor strikes in the city previously, but this was the first one where labor leaders clearly and unambiguously pointed to the color line in the workplace as a right enjoyed by white workers.[27]

Race and the workplace would come to a head again during the summer of 1916 when African American workers at Seaboard Air Line struck for higher wages and better working conditions, and the company responded by hiring black replacement workers.[28] The fired workers did not remain idle but instead gathered at a labor recruiter's office the next day. The local sheriff moved to close any and all offices recruiting black labor. Black crowds gathered and demonstrated against the closings after the Seaboard strike and the Mayor J.E.T. Bowden ordered them arrested for vagrancy.[29]

When the activities of these labor agents came to light, city and business leaders publicly begged black labor to remain. The Trade and Labor Council found this action outrageous because they claimed that there was enough white labor in the city for local businesses to employ. But local management wanted to keep black labor around at all costs since they were a cheaper source of labor. In editorials the *Artisan* blamed white business and political leaders for turning their backs on white labor and pointed to the racial hypocrisy of capitalism, claiming that industry leaders were the most adamant in advocating the segregation of the races on the streetcars yet have no problem sitting next to black chauffeurs or servants in their cars. They went on to complain that cheap black labor created their luxurious lifestyles and enormous fortunes. The complexities of the labor situation took an unusual turn the next summer when a white labor agent was arrested for trying to contract white labor in the city. The *Artisan*, Jacksonville's labor newspaper, lambasted the chief of police for using threatening tactics commonly reserved for blacks. The headline read, "Intimidating White Men: Chief of Police Threatening White Men as he Did Negroes." When the police used these tactics on white recruiters and workers it brought condemnation from white labor leaders proving that vagrancy laws were understood to only apply to blacks and not whites.[30]

As the labor movement locally and in the state turned its back on black workers, blacks turned to the federal government to address racial grievances at the workplace. In 1920, black cleaning women from Jacksonville, employed by the Pullman Railroad Company, petitioned the United States Railroad Administration Women's Service over a series of grievances. The union that represented these black workers organized black men and women in the same locals, unlike most white unions. Bessie Paul and Betty Span both temporarily worked unskilled jobs, such as sewing pillows, for which the Pullman Railroad Company paid them at the lower unskilled rate. They demanded that since they were skilled laborers, and Paul a forewoman, they should have been paid at their higher pay scale while performing the unskilled duties. The Railroad Administration agreed and petitioned the Chicago headquarters of the company on their behalf, which resulted in both of them receiving back pay. In the same complaint a number of other unionized black women cleaners asked the Railroad Administration to take action against their substandard living conditions. They stated that the company provided a toilet equipped with a sandbox that the Railroad Administration agreed was too close in proximity to the white male and black male toilets. The Railroad Administration noticed that "The toilet is very poorly located near the colored men's and the white men's toilet. The entrance to each is screened."[31] The Railroad Administration recommended that the company look into moving the black women's toilet away from the sight of men since the screen door gave black women no privacy.[32] Although white union leaders as well as most white Floridians did not recognize black women as "ladies," the Federal Government by way of the Railroad Administration did concede that fact.

Table 6. Manufacturing sector of Duval County, 1860–1920

Year	Manufacturing Establishments	Employees
1860	17	214
1870	105	739
1880	44 (average)	597 (average)
1890	190	1,245
1900	214	2,292 (average)
1920	288 (average)	12,378 (average)

Note: Database excludes manufacturing/employee data for 1910.
Source: Historical Census Browser. Retrieved 4 March 2012 from the University of Virginia Geospatial and Statistical Data Center, http://www.fisher.lib.virginia.edu/collections/stats/histcensus/index.html.

On 26 December 1918, twenty-one black porters employed by the Florida East Coast Railway filed a complaint with the Department of Labor's Division of Negro Economics because earlier that year, the department had warned railway companies that they could no longer force porters to perform duties reserved for flagmen, brakemen, and conductors. This was a practice used by railroad companies to exploit black unskilled labor in skilled positions because the skilled jobs were reserved for whites.[33] During the war the expanded interventionist government provided a new outlet for African American workers—especially railroad workers whose industry was viewed as crucial to the war effort. Porters documented company violations and demanded either back pay for the additional duties or formal promotion to the skilled positions with a commensurate increase in pay, neither of which the Division of Negro Economics eventually supported.[34] The labor shortage during the war created an opportunity for black men who entered the workforce. However, workplace practices on the part of employers and labor leaders kept black workers from enjoying any social and economic mobility attached to the new opportunities. Even though the Florida State Federation of Labor (FSFL) ignored black workers and their demands during this time, these cases represent the many instances of black railroad workers turning to the federal government during this time for help in negotiating workplace grievances that harkened back to the days of the Civil War era Freedmen's Bureau.[35]

By the end of World War I, blacks did not create a mass exodus out of the labor movement—however, it was clear that through official channels, rhetoric, and newspapers black workers did not enjoy the same place in the local labor movement that they did during the 1902 carpenter's strike. Similar to the public sphere, blacks were pushed out of labor's counterpublic to that of a voiceless observer. Issues that could provide a common ground to both black and white workers, much less any concerns that centered on race and racial discrimination, would have no place in the labor movement of the 1910s. In fact, during World War I, black workers were successful in bypassing the labor movement entirely and petitioning the federal government to address racial discrimination at the workplace.

8

Women's Counterpublic

A women's counterpublic evolved differently than labor's counterpublic. Although black workers were the founders of the local labor movement, white and black women created parallel movements that rarely intersected privately or publicly. As with white labor leaders, when woman's suffrage emerged in the public sphere, white middle-class women evoked white supremacy and privilege in their public demands for the franchise. Middle-class white women could not articulate a political message in the public sphere unless it was couched in their opposition to black uplift and equality. Since black women were not members in the woman's clubs or suffrage organization with white women, their counterpublic was racially exclusive but merged with a broader black counterpublic where black men and women could meet. This did not stop black women from organizing a counterpublic that engaged the dominant public sphere in many of the same ways as white women. Although black women organized clubs and organizations exclusively for black women, when it came to suffrage and civil rights, these organizations included both black men and women, and the rights of black women as a sex usually took a backseat to the rights of black women as a race.

Women entered the public sphere in the city by the late nineteenth century. Although evidence of women's participation does not emerge until the end of the century, both Edward Ayers and Elsa Barkley Brown have observed elsewhere in the South, both white and black women probably publicly and privately participated in political culture earlier. In 1888, the *Florida Times-Union* stated that black women lined up at polling locations to support black men and the Republican candidates in that specific election. A Northern reporter for *Outlook* magazine witnessed white men and women attending a political rally to support the third-party candidate in the November 1893 election. The reporter observed that "the [white] women are as much interested and as fully alive to the political situation as the men." This reporter even noted that while sitting in back of the church he noticed "several sunbonnets would turn around to me and the fine strong faces underneath glow with feelings as they nodded their approval or disapproval to me."[1]

Middle-class white women in Jacksonville took a further step into the public sphere with the formation of the Jacksonville Woman's Club in 1896. Inspired by and modeled on the Atlanta Woman's Club, the club met each week in the Windsor Hotel during this time. In a speech to the club in 1897, Katherine L. Eagan explained how the club was an important step as a tool of public engagement by stating:

> Some one has said that "organization is civilization." It is certainly true that wherever the [white] race has advanced it has been along the lines of organization. . . . It is not simply a craze that is sweeping women into clubs and societies. It is the trend of our age a desire to keep in touch with other [white] women who are thinking and acting independently. Twenty years ago the social relations even of people of means, were largely determined by their religious and political sympathies and were limited to the churches which the women openly attended and to the party with which the men of the family voted.[2]

Eagan was optimistic that the Jacksonville Woman's Club would force women to engage with other white women outside of their "own kind or set." Although not overtly political or even addressing the franchise, the club sought to organize activities around "social, literary and humanitarian" activities. Even though their charter forbade any political party advocacy, they did not shy away from the political when in the 1898 program a quote from Anna Elizabeth Dickinson, who was a Northern abolitionist and woman's suffrage advocate, was reproduced as "Exceptional Women Ought to Have Exceptional Rights." While created and nurtured in the private sphere, the club periodically engaged in the public sphere. The Jacksonville Woman's Club started with modest aims, but eventually it grew in size and ambition to include a legislative committee that lobbied local and state governments on a number of reforms including child labor, women prison reform, workplace regulations for women and children (such as petitioning Duval County government for the right of women to be elected to the School Board). The club was not only exclusive to the middle class, but also racially exclusive as it did not have black or even Jewish members. Jewish women created a Jewish Woman's League as did black women organize numerous women's clubs for their fraternal and charity work.[3]

White middle-class women engaged in the public sphere in very traditional ways during this time. In the spring of 1900 the *Metropolis* newspaper launched a "Woman's Edition" that featured a dozen middle-class white women as reporters who traveled throughout the city with "white badges, announcing that they had entered the trying and responsible occupation of reporters." The Jacksonville Woman's Club initiated this effort.[4] Earlier in the year the club took to the pages of the *Florida Times-Union* to publish a letter supporting candidates for the Board of Public Instruction. The club leaders were careful not to make their actions appear militant or provocative. At the end of their plea they stated:

> The Woman's Club does not propose to invade the realm of politics, but it feels a deep interest in the public schools, and makes this appeal to the voters feeling confident that they will support the club in this effort on behalf of the schools.[5]

The club objected to the board closing the schools a month early to save money. Club leaders organized members to teach white boys and girls during the month public schools were not operating. In the early years of the Jacksonville Woman's Club, club women hosted distinguished speakers in a public lectures series. One in 1898 featured Duncan U. Fletcher, who spoke at great length on the history of the legal and political rights of women dating back to the constitutional rights in English common laws. Fletcher concluded that "the position [white] women occupies [*sic*] under the law . . . seems hardly consistent with the advance of the sex in the present day."[6]

White women in other parts of the South, such as Baltimore, Mississippi, and Tennessee, formed early efforts for suffrage and petitioned state governments for women's suffrage. Many women from the South also attended national suffrage conferences before state and local suffrage chapters emerged.[7] In Florida, while woman's clubs emerged throughout the urban centers, the state suffrage movement began in 1893 in Tampa through the organizing of a white woman named Ella C. Chamberlin. She created the Florida Woman Suffrage Association and wrote articles about suffrage for a local newspaper. Chamberlin and other white women grew the organization to over one hundred people who decried the fact that "aliens and negroes" had participated in elections and white women did not. Chamberlin and other white women from the Tampa area also attended national suffrage conventions yearly until 1897 when Chamberlin left the state and her nascent organization grew silent without her. Women suffrage did not get a state voice again until June 1912 when thirty white women in Jacksonville organized a branch of the Equal Franchise League that started an eight-year campaign for white woman's suffrage in the state. Florida followed other Southern states during a second wave of Southern suffrage beginning in 1910 due to the success of women in Northern states and overseas in Britain.[8]

The middle-class white women's counterpublic formed out of the private spaces of the Jacksonville Woman's Club. In hotels and the private parlors of homes a discussion of suffrage and political rights were not uncommon. The club hosted Laura Clay—an official with the National Women's Equal Rights Association in the fall of 1910. That same year the club read and discussed Florence Kelley's book *Some Ethical Gains through Legislation*. The club even sponsored debates on local government, municipal ownership, the benefits of socialism, and the legal status of married women in Florida. Equal Franchise League meetings and events were announced at club meetings as were coordinating lobbying and other activities. However, the club refused to endorse woman's suffrage officially or publicly, as it was believed to violate the prohibition on "political matters" according to their constitution and bylaws.[9]

Immediately the league started a public campaign for white women's suffrage. The organization had important benefactors in the likes of James

J. Heard, the president of Heard National Bank. He provided them with free space in the Heard Bank Building on the corners of Forsyth and Laura streets in a room on the first floor with windows overlooking the sidewalk. The league painted on their window "Florida Equal Franchise League" alongside "Votes for Women." The league edited a special edition of the muckraking paper the *State,* which league leaders referred to as "a grand piece of propaganda." The Florida Equal Franchise League professed to focus its efforts and energies on introducing an "amendment to the Constitution of Florida granting to one half of her Caucasian population their inherent right of full citizenship." As Marjorie Spruill Wheeler noted, Southern white women during this time believed they were superior to blacks and thus felt slighted that black men constitutionally enjoyed the vote and not them.[10]

There was a great deal of crossover between the Jacksonville Woman's Club and the Equal Franchise League. Eagan was elected president at the first meeting at the home of Elizabeth B. Anderson. Eagan and Anderson publicly chastised critics who likened their organizing to "fun-making." Eagan emphatically declared that the organization was years in the planning after study of the national suffrage movement and assisted through the woman's club, where many were active members. Through discussions within the club concerning lobbying for legislation, only then did these women decide to form a separate organization for "the purpose of furthering [white] women's place in the affairs of the government." At this first meeting Eagan likened white women's strict relegation to the "home sphere" to that of slavery and insisted that women had the right to put "variety in her life [including] a study of politics and government." Two white men who attended this first meeting declared their intention of joining the organization. Out of fear that this public step forward would be interpreted as caustic and a disruption to the public spaces throughout the city, league leaders frequently declared that there was no desire "to engage in radical or militant strife," but would be an organization to educate women and men on the value of white women's suffrage.[11]

Between the Jacksonville Woman's Club and Florida Equal Franchise League, white middle-class women inserted themselves into a number of local and state political issues. One of the most important issues was that of child labor reform. In March 1913, the league hosted a conference on child labor at the St. James Building and invited suffrage activists to speak about the intersection of reform and suffrage. One speaker mentioned

Figure 12. *Throng of children trying to get into the already crowded theatre at Jacksonville while the Child Labor program was in session*, 1913. Photograph by Lewis Wickes Hine, Library of Congress.

that "[white] women must protect the women and children from the busy and thoughtless commercialism [and] must put into office men who will think along lines for the conservation of human health and human life."[12] White middle-class women even found common ground with the FSFL who too advocated for child labor reform, equal pay for the sexes, and suffrage. John H. Mackey, the first vice president of the FSFL, stated that "it is a duty that devolves upon all men of this country to place them [white women] upon an equal footing, so far as the ballot is concerned."[13]

In the 1915 municipal elections, middle-class white women took a public stand in the mayor's race. Incumbent mayor, Van C. Swearingen, was able to draw over three thousand people in Hemming Park for a rally. The *Metropolis* stated that the rally was organized by the local "women's movement." Although movement leaders organized the event, none spoke to the crowd. The speakers not only showed their support for the mayor, but also praised white women for participating in the event. When Fred B. Noble spoke to the crowd he asked that "the voter stand by them [white women] in their aspirations to elevate the moral welfare of the city." Soon after being elected into office in 1913, Swearingen began a campaign to move all illicit businesses such as gambling and prostitution to a "restricted district" on the west end of downtown on Bridge and Ward streets.[14] Carolina Hallowes Barnett was the only woman who spoke. At the end she thanked the crowd for "its expression in turning out to assist the movement of the women in behalf of Mayor Swearingen." In the 1915 mayor's race, white women stepped into the public sphere like never before to campaign for a specific candidate. Swearingen lost reelection to J.E.T. Bowden. But in the town of Fellsmere, Florida, Zena M. Dreier was the first woman to cast a vote in a municipal election in the South when officials changed the city charter. This milestone did not go unnoticed in Jacksonville.[15]

The Equal Franchise League periodically brought a number of speakers to Jacksonville to give talks about suffrage. Their speakers brought with them a number of opposing views. Florence Kelley was a white Northern suffrage organizer, settlement-house worker, socialist, and member of the NAACP. She spoke jointly with Jeane Gordon a white Southern suffrage organizer from New Orleans. Gordon and Kelley were in the city to attend the 1913 Child Labor Conference. Kelley and Gordon represented two very different approaches to the suffrage debate. Kelley advocated suffrage through national action by way of federal legislation or amendment, what the meeting referred to as the "London manner." Although Kelley might have been racially liberal she placated the crowd by referring to Reconstruction as the time when the country suffered due to the "large ignorant [black men] vote cast upon the country" while "disfranchising Southern white men at the same time." Local women were more interested in Gordon's approach, which represented a "States' Rights" policy regarding suffrage.

Gordon was asked to return the following year where she mapped out her political strategy in greater detail. She believed an amendment to the U.S. Constitution would be vetoed by Southern lawmakers as a bloc, and instead it was up to Southern women to educate lawmakers in state houses. Gordon continued that "if we are able to educate the people up to the point where they will vote to give women their rights there will be no need of an amendment to the Federal Constitution."[16]

The Equal Suffrage League decided to pursue a States' Rights approach and petition lawmakers in Tallahassee. During the 1913 legislative session

H. L. Bussey of Palm Beach County introduced a resolution calling for a constitutional amendment granting women the right to vote. Although Bussey introduced the idea to the State House, he had little faith in the principle stating he opposed giving the right to vote to "rockers of the cradle." White middle-class women from Jacksonville traveled to Tallahassee to lobby for the resolution and publicly show their support for it. Florence Murphy Cooley remarked how "seats were filled, aisles were filled, the steps of the Speaker's rostrum were filled, windows had people standing in them and in the hall as far as one could see, people were standing on chairs to hear the first call for the rights of women, ever uttered in the Capital of the State." What these women did not expect was to be stymied by their own House representative from Duval County, St. Elmo W. "Chic" Acosta. Speaking from the floor of the House, Acosta challenged the legitimacy of the delegation and the role of women in the public sphere.[17]

The Duval County representative wanted to cast these women as aberrations and just part of a minority of white women out to disrupt the social order of the South. Acosta claimed that since these women traveled to Tallahassee, they must have abandoned their responsibilities to the home in order to lobby House members. He concluded that these women were "either single women, or married women without children, who wouldn't have children." For him a woman was not respectable unless she remained in the private sphere of the home. He singled out Francis Anderson specifically from the House floor and accused her father of not voting for him but for the Bull Moose Party in 1912. Not only was he suggesting she and her family were not even Democrats, but she was not to be considered a political agent on her own but subject to her father. Although women believed they were traveling to Tallahassee to engage in the theatre of the public sphere, Acosta too used the moment for performance. Grace Locke observed:

He was on the platform with us, and his continual winks to various members on the floor, his grimaces half-concealed and openly made, the shakes of his head when statements were made, his half-mumbled audible utterances derogatory to the facts adduced—his whole general manner during the time the bill was under consideration were the most discourteous to say the least I have ever seen a women receive in the South.[18]

The delegation interpreted Acosta's winks, smiles, and other mannerisms as evidence that he did not take them seriously and thought their efforts were no better than "fun-making."

Acosta went to another familiar trope—that of the "lost cause"—to call the suffrage effort illegitimate. Acosta stated that suffrage was not indigenous to the South or even Jacksonville but part of some "Northern invasion." He leveled against the "North" a series of transgressions when he stated,

> The Yankees came to our fair State and devastated it, laying low the homes of our people and freeing our negroes. We receive the freezes from the North which destroy our groves and crops. We receive financial depression which comes from the North and destroys our business interests. And now the Suffragettes, who come from the North, seek to destroy our homes, separating man from his wife, while the children grow up like weeds in the forest.[19]

Acosta called the bill "dangerous" and claimed that its passage would result in some public riot, chaos, or other disorder as experienced in England where the suffrage activists and their office was attacked by a mob. This was a way to suggest that white women could not germinate a social movement on their own, and the threat was that these women were moving away from the calming and civilizing influences of their husbands and fathers by radical white women from the North. The reason for this suggestion was that Jeannette Rankin, field secretary for the National American Woman's Suffrage Association, joined the Tallahassee delegation. Rankin was insulted by the slight and replied later to reporters that "[i]n suffrage States a working woman is respected as to her feelings and is treated as an equal. I know 'chivalry' covers the 'ladies' of the South; and now I am sure there is work for the movement to give the honest working women equality in Florida." Rankin accused Acosta of equating suffrage activism and engagement in the public sphere with disrobing the virtues of being a "lady." Rankin questioned whether Acosta did not want his Northern (presumably male) friends to spend their winters in Florida since that too was a "Northern invasion."[20]

The bill was defeated in the House by thirteen votes. Upon their return the delegation promised to fight against Acosta and other likeminded politicians and furnish the "flowers for some political corpses." A week later the delegation returned to Tallahassee to lobby the Senate to pass the same measure. White women gathered in the public spaces around the Senate and chanted, "Don't look like 'Chic!' Don't get like 'Chic!' Don't be like 'Chic!' Rah, rah, rah! Equal Suffrage!" Equal Franchise League leaders stated this second delegation had the mission to convince legislators that women in Florida were "clamoring for the vote, [and] that in Florida the movement is native; that it is urged by mothers and daughters of Southern birth and rearing." League leaders acknowledged that these rallies were in effect a "hearing before the people who are the real power—the voters." In this second rally white women reminded men that not only is the practice of citizenship and the franchise connected to the rights of "manhood," but exercising it fairly and judiciously was the true measure of a manly virtue.[21]

The second delegation stayed five weeks lobbying state senators to support the bill and was joined by white women from throughout the state. Conscious of the two decades–long struggle to disfranchise black men, the delegation tried to convince legislators that white women were not interested in voting as a bloc or participating in fusion tickets or voting for independent candidates. They reported having the hardest time meeting with their own senators from Duval County, who refused the delegation and eventually voted against the bill. Senators from Escambia County, where none of the delegates originated, gave public support for the effort and voted as such. This left such an impression on the delegation that Locke promised to start a campaign for Escabmia's John P. Stokes for governor. The bill was defeated in the Senate by one vote. When the delegation returned they claimed the narrow margin in the Senate as evidence of "not defeat but victory," and promised to educate voters throughout the state on the virtues of white women's suffrage. To facilitate this effort club women in Jacksonville helped to organize a Florida Suffrage League at the annual meeting of the Florida Federated Women's Club in Orlando that November. The Florida Equal Suffrage League voted to change its name to the Jacksonville Equal Suffrage League in 1916 and affiliate with the Florida Equal Suffrage Association as a single statewide voice.[22]

Between 1913 and 1919 the Equal Franchise League organized and lobbied each session of the legislature for a suffrage amendment. In public meetings held throughout the city the league brought in national speakers—both white men and women—to talk about white women's suffrage. This was part of their education campaign and became very public events. There was no admission and the white public was welcomed and encouraged to attend. Musical programs accompanied the events and in 1915 league women screened the silent film *Your Girl and Mine*, which was based on a suffrage play. Speakers spoke at length at the success made outside the South in regard to woman's suffrage in states like Ohio. National speakers shared the stage with local white suffrage leaders with the current president of the Equal Franchise League presiding over the events.[23]

During the 1917 state legislative session, Equal Franchise League leaders scored a victory in that a woman was allowed to speak to a joint session of the legislature as opposed to having white men speak for them or lobbying politicians personally. May Mann Jennings, wife of former governor William S. Jennings, delivered a speech in support of the state suffrage amendment.[24] Upon leaving the governor's office the Jennings moved to Jacksonville, and May Jennings became an office holder with the Jacksonville Woman's Club. Jennings argued that "giving the ballot to the [white] women makes her a better wife and mother, fits her for more thoroughly training her children in the duties of citizenship and brings about a closer comradeship between husband and wife." Jennings asserted that the private family sphere would not suffer if women were given full access to the public sphere. Although it was reported that Jennings was "frequently applauded" the legislature still refused to move on women's suffrage.[25]

While many Equal Franchise League events engaged in a mannerly discourse on the nature of white women's suffrage, league leaders were not beyond symbolic theatre to engage the public. On 9 February 1919 the league sponsored an event at the Morocco Temple called "the Suffrage Prison Special Party." This was an event touring the country during this time. Women from around the country as well as locals dressed in prison costumes and told the stories of women who were arrested for agitating for the right to vote. What made this event remarkable was that every woman on the program advocated and supported the Susan B. Anthony Amendment before the U.S. Congress. This represented an abandonment of the States' Rights approach of the Florida suffrage movement in favor of a national solution. Not only were speakers and performers at the party event engaging locals about suffrage, but also Congress, the Senate, and President Woodrow Wilson. Months later the amendment was passed and ratified, making 1920 the first year women could vote in Jacksonville.[26]

Always at issue with woman's suffrage was the race question. Both Marjorie Spruill Wheeler and Elna C. Green conclude that appealing to the virtues of white supremacy did not provide incentive to Southern Democrats who successfully disfranchised black votes already. The Equal Franchise League was formed for the express purpose to garner half of the "Caucasian population" with the vote. The city's muckraking paper *Dixie* chimed in on the question of race and suffrage when it ran an editorial stating that the only way the state can support woman's suffrage was through adopting a grandfather clause to the state constitution that would eliminate not only black women but the remaining black men who still voted. White women in the suffrage movement imagined their condition in relation to blacks in the South.

On 9 May 1917, the National Woman's Party sponsored a banquet at the Seminole Hotel in Jacksonville that included a number of national speakers. The banquet addressed the race question. White Northern suffrage activist Alice Paul spoke to the crowd arguing that "since Congress had given the negro, the Porto [*sic*] Rican and other aliens the right of voting with the American white man that the [white] women felt certain that they deserved at least as much, if not more, consideration at the hands of the lawmakers of the nation." At the same event, Ella St. Clair Thompson, a white suffrage activist from North Carolina, made the case that the only way poor whites could be uplifted was through white women voting en masse. She commented that the children of poor black washerwomen were able to receive an education, while the children of poor whites in the South work twelve hours a day in the cotton mills without access to fresh air, an education, and any other civilizing advancement. She chastised the opponents of suffrage by stating that "men need the good white women of the South to help you solve this problem." Thompson then referred to prostitution as the "white slave problem" and commented that women needed the vote to "protect her and her sisters' interests."[27] Suffrage activists were very careful to construct a rhetoric that was exclusive to only white women and tied white racial uplift on the back of white woman's suffrage.

While white middle class women emerged in the public sphere, black middle class women followed suit in a similar fashion. Both Evelyn Brooks Higginbotham and Rosalyn Terborg-Penn tell us that black women's club experience would prepare them for the suffrage movement.[28] Unfortunately, there is scant evidence of these activities and the white newspapers published little in regard to black club women activities as compared to white. In the 1910s, black women formed the City Federation of Colored

Figure 13. Margaret Murray Washington shown visiting a black public school in Jacksonville, March 1913. William R. Cole, University of North Florida, Special Collections.

Women's Clubs. Unlike the Jacksonville Woman's Club, the Colored Women's Club was an association composed of numerous smaller organizations run by black women. Clubs included the Phillis Wheatly Club, Mary Church Terrell Club, Improvement Club, Mother's Club, and the L. C. Fleming Club along with numerous aid societies and church groups, all run by black women. In March 1913, the Colored Women's Club hosted a debate between Margaret Murray Washington, the wife of Booker T. Washington, and Lillian A. Turner—both of whom were officers of the National Association of Colored Women. The meeting was held at Bethel Baptist Institutional Church. And with only the program remaining it is hard to know what was discussed at the meeting, but Washington typically promoted her husband's accommodation policies concerning the race question and Turner was a well-known speaker on black woman's suffrage and was listed as providing the response to Washington's position. It is conceivable that this debate addressed the role of black women and the suffrage question.[29]

Colored women's clubs and their white counterparts could find common ground in the private spaces of the club for interracial dialogue and action as they did in places like North Carolina. In 1916, Mattie Simmons, chair of the legislative committee of the Jacksonville Woman's Club, gave an address to the Colored Women's Club, which probably included the ways in which the woman's club engaged in the public sphere. She was one of six white women from the club to speak to the Colored Women's Club that year. The Jacksonville Woman's Club noted in the minutes that as a result of these interracial meetings they learned that the Colored Women's Club was "doing splendid work for the women of their race." The Colored Women's Club also engaged overtly in the public sphere by posting signs in public places to remind black men to pay the poll tax and register to vote. They met with county commissioners to advocate for prison reform including better ventilation and installing a chapel for religious services—all of which they received. The Colored Women's Club sponsored activities that engaged in the public sphere such as committee titles that included Civic, Good Roads, Juvenile Court, and Suffrage.[30]

Probably the most important woman to these organizations during this time was Eartha M. M. White. Not only was she active in numerous black women-led organizations like the Colored Women's Club, she also led organizations that joined black men and women in a common mission. She was president of the Colored Citizen's Protective League in 1903. She also spoke as a featured speaker to the Duval County Central Republican Club. White personally went before the Jacksonville Board of Trade to ask for help in supporting what would become the "Colored Old Folks Home." Not only did the president of the Board of Trade, Charles Edwin Garner, express his support to her effort in a letter from the board, but so did Governor William S. Jennings as well as other board members who wrote personal notes of support to White on the margins of the letter.[31]

In 1913 White was selected as president of the Lincoln Memorial Association. That year the organization under her leadership celebrated the fifty years of the Emancipation Proclamation. This was a celebration of not only President Abraham Lincoln but also Frederick Douglass. The "Guests of Honor" really spoke to the ways in which these associations could bring different political actors to the same venue. James Weldon Johnson, native son and field secretary of the NAACP was a featured guest, as was Joseph E. Lee, the old Republican warhorse and Reconstruction Era judge. William S. Jordan, the sitting mayor of Jacksonville, was included as a guest of honor to demonstrate the pull someone like White had to fill out the venue. The program addressed the place of blacks in America fifty years after the Emancipation Proclamation. Students from Stanton sang "Long Live Lincoln" and the event closed with everyone in attendance singing the hymn "Blessed Be the Ties that Bind," which speaks to Christian fellowship and unity. And being that the event was created to celebrate the political emancipation of blacks from slavery, the hymn was probably chosen for its message of collective plight in adversity. Speechmakers spoke on topics such as "Fifty Years of Educational Progress" and "Fifty Years of Freedom." Although the program was meant to reflect on a past milestone, it certainly represented an opportunity to look forward.[32]

Eartha M. M. White was not unusual for black women in Jacksonville. Margaret D. McCleary was the secretary for the local NAACP branch during 1917. Like White, she was an officer and organizer for an organization that included black men and women and was the point of contact for the national office of the NAACP during her tenure. Like the Colored Women's Club, the NAACP engaged in the public sphere with various degrees of success. In November 1917 the NAACP held a meeting and celebration at the Laura Street Presbyterian Church, where Mary McLeod Bethune gave the address that evening. The occasion was a celebration of the Buchanan v. Warley Supreme Court decision that declared residential segregation unconstitutional. The branch was newly chartered and used the celebration to set an agenda for the coming year. Like the Jacksonville Woman's Club, black women directly engaged with local officials concerning policy matters. McCleary petitioned the Board of Education to institute reforms so black schools could operate equally to white schools including a summer training program for black teachers and equal pay to white teachers. McCleary indicated in her report to the national office that the board welcomed her and invited her to come back with any more concerns. McCleary was also important in getting the NAACP involved in criminal court cases where black defendants were mistreated or abused by local police officers. She found defense attorneys for them and reported their cases to the black press and national office.[33]

While in the private sphere African American women had greater opportunities to hold leadership positions in these types of intersex organizations than their white counterparts, it did not translate into the ability to maneuver through the black counterpublic with ease. McCleary tried

Figure 14. Margaret Murray Washington and Eartha M. M. White with women of the City Federation of Colored Women's Clubs of Jacksonville, 1913. Photograph by William R. Cole. University of North Florida, Special Collections.

to organize a protest march called the Silent Parade to protest the East Saint Louis Race Riot of 1917. James Weldon Johnson tried to privately coordinate local branches to organize parades simultaneously with the national organization in New York. McCleary reported to Johnson that at a meeting to vote on the Silent Parade, older black men such as W. I. Lewis and George H. Mays admonished the attendees over such a provocative act. She claimed that Lewis "came to register a strong kick" and Mays "placed a very effectual wet blanket over everybody's enthusiasm." Resistance to the Silent Parade was not only internally contentious: word of this organizing within the private spaces of the counterpublic found its way to the mayor's office and McCleary got wind that the mayor's office was hesitant to provide permits and the police were unwilling to provide protection since race relations had deteriorated over the previous year.[34]

Black women and their place in the South were integrated with their position as a subject race in the region. In a letter to James Weldon Johnson, McCleary was taken aback that he would use the term "you all" because of its association as a Southern phrase. She informed him that she always used "all of you" or the plural "you" as to not be regarded as a "Southerner."[35] This was a far cry from the white suffrage activists who publicly placed their movement in the "lost cause" and states' rights. Mc-Cleary contextualized these events more broadly than her white counterparts. For her, work in the NAACP was more akin to the French Revolution. McCleary described the political movement for blacks and what was at stake:

> The general tension down here reminds me very much of the causes and feelings which led up to, or rather, caused the French Revolution as given us by Alexander Dumas. But is it not true that any race of people who have wrenched from their oppressors their inalienable rights have had to do so by the greatest sacrificed and sufferings? Must we not prepare to also pay the price?[36]

Middle-class white women used the idea of the "home" and their moral compass as the political argument for their entry into suffrage. Black middle-class women did not have the luxury to be that provincial in their political ambitions since they were working toward racial liberation.

Almost all of the black women who joined the NAACP listed their occupation as "housewife." McCleary's husband was a doctor and not unlike white club and suffrage women, enjoyed middle-class backgrounds. Since there was no expectation of black women being deferential to their fathers and husbands as white women, they could enjoy a more egalitarian role in these organizations than what white middle-class women experienced. It also should be noted that white women's organizations used the individual or singular "woman" to describe themselves, while black organizations used the plural "women." White women had to present themselves as no threat to the white male power structure in the city, and so they advocated for the uplift of women individually. Black women instead wanted to project their singularity of purpose and their desire for unity, so their organizations were "colored women" associations. Black women had the latitude to be more racially confrontational than black men or white women, who merely prodded white men about their "manly" virtues.[37]

Although middle-class white women's counterpublic was distinct from the dominant public sphere, black women freely participated in the black counterpublic. Since black men and women shared a common threat to freely accessing the franchise and since black women were not regarded as "ladies" by the white dominant public sphere, black women and their political discourse could be integrated into the black counterpublic. White women had to reason and articulate with white men as to why their political discourse deserved to be considered as part of the dominant public sphere. The race question became the central justification for middle-class white women to argue for free and unfettered access to the public sphere and the franchise itself.

Conclusion

The Black Counterpublic Comes of Age

The black counterpublic evolved over time in Jacksonville. As spaces in the city became less democratized, the opportunities and desire for blacks to join the public sphere openly also decreased. So much so that when the black counterpublic engaged the dominant public it appeared spontaneous and often times caustic as with the cases of the Jacksonville riot of 1892 and streetcar boycotts. However, these moments were not spontaneous but were the result of covert planning and organizing. Between the summer of 1919 and fall of 1920, Jacksonville residents witnessed the black counterpublic engage the public sphere unlike any time before in its history. The lynching that occurred in 1919, the FSFL conference the following year, and the election of 1920 were the causative agents and the loci for the black counterpublic to become transgressive to the dominant public sphere.

Although the city of Jacksonville tried hard to uphold its reputation as a Southern community without a lynching, Duval County would record

Table 7. Total population of Jacksonville, 1900–1920

Year	Total	White	Percent (%)	Black	Percent (%)
1900	28,429	12,158	42	16,236	57
1910	57,699	28,329	49	29,293	50
1920	91,558	46,078	50	41,520	45

Source: Bureau of the Census, *Census of Population*, 1900–1920.

its first on 9 May 1909. Few details have survived other than that an un-named black man was accused to have attacked one Mrs. John Deas on her farm roughly fifteen miles from Jacksonville. When the sheriff came to the scene the suspect was already dead, and the sheriff "could get no information as to the identity of those in the mob."[1] This incident sounded an ominous tone in that the successes of the 1890s to keep lynch parties at bay were breaking down.

Urban violence and riots prefaced the summer of 1919, an especially turbulent year in American racial history. African American migration to urban areas had increased steadily, heightening racial tensions. Chicago, Knoxville, and Omaha experienced huge "race riots."[2] In the spring of 1919 two high-profile lynchings in Madison and Milton saw Florida Governor Sidney J. Catts and the national office of the NAACP exchange heated letters publicly over the state's commitment to protect black suspects in custody. Catts came across as a defender of the lynch mob when he confessed that "If any man, white or black, should dishonor one of my family he would meet my pistol square from the shoulder, and every white man in this South, who is a red-blooded American, feels the same as I do."

Anticipating a summer of racial tension, Jacksonville's white business-men and local politicians made a plea for "harmony," because the Florida Purchase Centennial Exposition was considering Jacksonville as the site for the state fair during the summer of 1919. Believing this would bring added business and attention, they wanted to ensure tranquility and of course calm race relations. They stated, "Harmony must prevail. . . . and it must be meet [*sic*] with the fullest and heartiest cooperation from all persons."[3]

Earlier that summer, police had found two black hack drivers mur-dered. Other drivers believed that the killings evidenced antiblack violence, since the last passengers of the murdered men had been white and their bodies were found in a white neighborhood. Protesting the lack of police cooperation in solving the cases, black drivers refused to carry white passengers.[4]

Early on the evening of 20 August, two African American drivers refused service to George Du Bose, a prominent white insurance manager with customers in several black neighborhoods. The drivers told Du Bose that they were no longer providing service to white customers. This refusal was part of an organized boycott because a number of black hack drivers were found murdered while the police refused to investigate. Du Bose argued and pulled a gun from his coat. A large African American crowd gathered. Du Bose fired shots into the mob but did not injure anyone. The crowd retaliated with rocks and other objects. By the time the police arrived, Du Bose was dead. Du Bose was a descendent of a prominent Jacksonville family, and his brother was a sitting judge at the time. Those who witnessed the event from their windows refused to help police.[5]

Later that evening, the police questioned all African American cab drivers and eventually charged John Morine and Bowman Cook with murder.[6] Leading black citizens immediately released a statement to the *Florida Times-Union*. Fearful of white mob action, they called for swift and equitable justice and offered assistance in the investigation, reiterating white businessmen's pleas for law and order. For three days, the sheriff swore in special deputies and police to prevent mob violence.[7] A lynch mob or other related violence did not immediately emerge in the day following the arrest of Morine and Cook.

As the Du Bose hysteria seemed to die down, the police arrested Ed Jones, an African American, for allegedly assaulting a thirteen-year-old white girl. The sheriff again feared mob violence; he personally took Jones to a jail in nearby St. Augustine.[8] Unaware of Jones's departure, a crowd of masked men broke open the jail doors and reportedly overpowered the only guard. When they could not find Jones, they referred to a written list and asked the jailer for Cook and Morine, who were still being held for the murder of Du Bose. The guard released both men to the crowd.[9] The lynch mob took the two hack drivers to the edge of town, where they shot them. The mob tied Cook's body to the back of a car and dragged it through the city streets while they dumped Morine's body in front of one of the more popular hotels.[10]

Some blacks believed that insurance agents led the mob, exacting re-venge for the murder of one of their own. Reverend John A. Gregg, presi-dent of Edward Waters College, believed it was city leaders who, if not directly responsible, assisted in quelling any investigation of the lynch-ing. He claimed that local officials were reading his mail. In a letter to Mary White Ovington of the NAACP, he wrote that he "feared that some are involved in the matter who are 'higher up,' and for some reason, al-though they have called the Grand Jury, we fear that no true bill will be returned." As an indication of who might be involved, the county solicitor went to Ashley Street where Du Bose met the cab and started to shoot indiscriminately in rage at the cabs there and then around the neighbor-hood. He was subsequently arrested.[11] Ironically, in the same week the Centennial Exposition Committee judges must have considered the inci-dents insignificant or as restoration of the racial order, because it selected Jacksonville as a fair site even though "harmony" was not engendered in the atmosphere during those weeks.

A grand jury investigation concluded that the lynching was a premedi-tated plot to avenge Du Bose's murder, although the actions of the mob demonstrated more concern for sending a message to the black commu-nity then avenging the death of Du Bose since Ed Jones was a target as well. Investigators criticized the sheriff's handling of the lynching, im-plying that he had played a role in lax judgment, albeit in their opinion negligible.[12]

The Chamber of Commerce, the Rotary Club, and the Kiwanis Club all publicly condemned the lynching; other groups claimed they wanted legal actions taken against the mob. Jacksonville's black organizations too brought attention to the lynching. The Local NAACP, Business Men's League, and the Branch for Law and Order jointly sent a telegram to Gov-ernor Catts, which stated that local blacks "have done and are doing all [they] can to apprehend the guilty parties, but at the same time we desire to say that we feel deeply this crime against Duval County and the fair City of Jacksonville that now places them in the column of other com-munities which have here-to-fore shown such utter disregard to law and order."[13]

The descent of Jacksonville since the 1890s was not lost on black lead-ers. John Gregg in a letter to the NAACP lamented that "the hoodlum element that perpetrated this crime took advantage of the better elements who had previously put down a lynching."[14] Gregg's conclusion was that for decades the affluent whites and city leaders kept the white working class from indulging in lynchings over the years. With the death of Du Bose who was from a patrician family and with racial tensions at an all-time high, the conditions were such that the lynching of the suspects in Du Bose's murder facilitated a common ground between these two groups.

Eighteen days after the lynching, a black man named Claude Howell hitched a ride with a group of other black men. Officer John Turknett suspected trouble and pulled the car over. Other officers harassed those in the car while Turknett followed Howell home, fired upon Howell before he reached the door, and wounded him. Howell fired back at Turknett, mortally wounding him.[15]

Howell escaped and took refuge in several sympathetic African American homes through the course of the evening. Police finally caught him the next morning. Although Howell pleaded self-defense, the police applied the "second degree" to get a "confession." Officials later told the press that Howell admitted that he shot Turknett not in self-defense but in a deliberate act of first-degree murder.[16]

Fearing another lynching, Howell was quickly given "due process." The presiding judge later bragged that this was the fastest murder trial in Florida history. Many African Americans, believing that Howell had been railroaded, protested his treatment and appeared at the trial to show their support. Before the jury announced the verdict, the justice ordered police to secure the courthouse after the guilty verdict and issued a sentence of death by hanging. The police arrested two African American men who publicly incited blacks to protest.[17]

Howell's case stirred up much anger within the African American community considering its hasty trial in the shadow of the lynching. Executions of black prisoners typically brought a crowd of blacks, more often than not those that prayed for the soul of the convicted. In an unusual move, many blacks showed up at his execution as a show of support, another symbolic and overt challenge to white supremacy and the verdict.[18]

Jacksonville's white leadership used the execution as propaganda. The *Metropolis* allegedly reported Howell's last statement, a literal plea for the races to work together for "harmony."[19] It seemed both ironic and ap-

Table 8. Men executed for murdering a law enforcement officer in Jacksonville, 1895–1919

Name of Convicted	Date of Offense	Date Sentenced	Time from Sentence to Execution
Alexander Simms	7 April 1895	27 May 1895	3 months, 3 days
Frank Roberson	26 June 1899	3 June 1902	1 year, 2 months, 4 days
Mose Roberson	26 June 1899	25 August 1899	2 years, 6 months, 10 days
Lonnie Rowland	15 September 1913	9 March 1914	10 months, 13 days
Claude Howell	26 September 1919	9 October 1919	8 days

Source: William Wilbanks, Forgotten Heroes: Police Officers Killed in Early Florida, 1840–1925, Paducah, Ky.: Turner Publishing Co., 1998.

propriate that the season began with a plea for harmony and ended with another plea for the very same thing.

The Morine and Cook lynching and the Howell execution marked a particularly violent year. In fact, blacks in Jacksonville became more defiant in the face of this violence. By early 1920, many of Jacksonville's blacks pulled insurance policies from white-owned companies and financed a black firm. The move was part of a boycott against the perceived perpetrators of the lynching. Articles published in black newspapers described the boycott not only to send a message to lynch mob leaders, but also to protest the treatment of blacks on streetcars and in polling booths. Eventually, white insurance companies turned to black agents to work segregated neighborhoods; and when entering black homes, white agents removed their hats and used "Mr." and "Mrs." as signs of respect.[20]

Although the lynching of 1919 was a spontaneous event, the actions of blacks before and after the lynching demonstrate the organizing of a black counterpublic below the surface of the public sphere. Everyday actions by blacks were statements born out of the counterpublic. The black counterpublic was manifest in the mobilizations of hack drivers to refuse service to white costumers, the pulling of insurance policies from white-owned companies, as well as the public support for Howell at his trial. This all represented a discourse on policing, the criminal justice system, and the vulgar impulses of white supremacy itself. The transgressive action of the lynchings—both legal and extralegal—was meant as a message broadcast in the public sphere for blacks to "stay in their place." However, their actions after these events demonstrate that this message was ignored.

In the spring of 1920 labor's counterpublic would confront the black counterpublic over the issue of race that had been boiling under the surface for years within the local movement. During the FSFL convention of 1920 in St. Augustine, two black union members from Jacksonville, T. J. Hankerson from the Carpenters Local 1972 and C. E. Todd from the Building Trades Council of Jacksonville, petitioned the body to formally join the meeting. By this time the AFL integrated the national meeting, which was interpreted as a symbolic move by black members—even if it did not produce any substantive change below. Having two blacks in attendance created quite a controversy within the meeting. The two black union members were asked to leave while the delegates debated whether to allow them to join the meeting. George M. Hull, representing the Central Trades and Labor Council of Jacksonville argued that since the AFL recognized no distinction based on race, the delegates should be allowed to join the convention.[21]

Several speakers from other parts of the state argued that by allowing the black members to join the meeting they would then be under the impression that they were equal to whites. One delegate who sympathized with the protest believed that it was important to organize black labor with the FSFL so there could be a more unified effort to address labor issues in the state. He believed that white supremacy would not be challenged if they were allowed to sit in the conference, because in the North whites and blacks did not enforce segregation, yet he believed blacks there did not press for racial equality as a result. A union delegate from Miami countered that even if whites in the convention make no issue of racial equality, the black delegates would assume their presence in the convention was an acknowledgment of racial equality, which was unacceptable. Upon further debate the black delegates were asked to leave, yet encouraged to organize on behalf of the labor cause in the state separately, striking a blow to meaningful interracial unionism.[22]

One black observer used this event to harshly criticize the FSFL in the following way:

The principle of united action for the elevation of labor seemed to have been lost in sight of the fear that the presence of the two colored delegates might in some way bring about "social equality" as if the Federation was a kind of *pink tea party* [author's emphasis].[23]

This observer imagining the annual FSFL meeting as a "pink tea party" should not be overlooked or dismissed because these tea parties were events civic or church "ladies" organized around a pink color theme, which were intended to include local residents for polite conversation. And since women were organizers and participants, any political talk would naturally be avoided.[24] What the observer was really saying was that if the FSFL was not going to address equality it might as well be a polite effeminate meeting of church women. In fact the observer went so far as to state that the FSFL embodied "a moral weakness" by not protecting the equal rights of the African American delegates at the meeting thus questioning their manhood for not standing up for racial equality.

It is hard to tell the organizing beforehand that brought these two delegates to the FSFL conference to demand an integrated meeting. Clearly this was part of a discourse in the way the actions that led to and followed the lynching of 1919 was part of a larger political discourse. Although this action was germinated out of the local labor movement's policies to push black workers to the margin of labor's counterpublic, the message at the center of this action was no different than others bore out of the black counterpublic about the rights of blacks as citizens.

No other event during this time really speaks to the actions of the black counterpublic and the white anxiety that it would engender than the election of 1920, when women across the country voted for the first time. In 1920 when black women organized for the presidential election fears of assertive black women took hold of whites. There was much anticipation when the primaries rolled around and women would be voting for the first time. Senator Duncan U. Fletcher gave a speech encouraging white women to register and vote. He was apprehensive due to the process by which it all happened. Advocating a States' Right approach, he conceded that the federal government has provided the authority to grant women the right to vote but feared the result would be similar as the last time this happened with the Fifteenth Amendment. He did not want to contest this and instead stated, "the matter is practically settled and I hope every white woman will qualify and vote in the coming primary as well as the general election." On 8 September 1920 Helen Hunt, president of the National Women's Party, became the first registered woman voter in Duval County.[25]

Helen Hunt notwithstanding, whites in the city soon feared a black revolt when they learned that black women were outnumbering white women in voter registrations. The headline of the *Metropolis* warned: "Democracy in Duval County Endangered by Very Large Registration Negro Women." It continued that "If White Men and White Women Do Not Awaken to New Political Situation, Negroes Will Wield Balance of Power in City and County." This was a quote from John E. Matthews, who was secretary of the Citizens' Registration Committee. Matthews claimed there was a "guiding hand" behind the number of black women organizing. It was reported that black women's organizations all required women to show their registration slips in order to participate in meetings and functions. Matthews went on to declare, "this is a white man's country and government, his by right and conquest by right of might, by right of blood he has spilt, and right of the brain and energy contributed to its building and development." Sherman Bryan Jennings wrote to his mother May Mann Jennings his concern that "we have more negro women registered than whites. . . . we will have some black councilwomen next time if the [white] women don't get out and register." White fears even crossed ethnic and religious lines when Rabbi Salo Stein encouraged Jewish women to register so that white women could help attain numerical superiority in the election. The scare tactics worked because by 7 October, white women had overtaken black women in total registrations and women of both races led men in total voter registrations, demonstrating how important this election was to women.[26]

White women formed the Duval County League of Democratic Women. They sponsored voting schools for white women, which not only assisted in registrations and directions on how to vote but local candidates also gave speeches and met white women voters at these places. The Duval County League also organized rallies throughout the city that featured speakers to help bring out the vote. To help intimidate black registrants, the city cracked down on "false registrations." The sheriff arrested Juanita Allen, a black woman who registration officials said lied about her age. The *Metropolis* tried to inflame the incident by saying black organizers threatened to kill the nineteen year old if she did not register. Blacks registering to vote were asked a number of questions about their personal lives as well as party affiliation and could be disqualified if they wavered or provided "false" information. Over five hundred warrants were issued by the sheriff's office to pursue blacks trying to register. This inspired Janice Lowder, a black women and organizer, to plead for the national offices of the NAACP to intervene because the newspapers "by publishing these statements of arresting these poor Colored women it is just to frightening [sic] them from the polls on election day." She claimed many black women confided in her that they were afraid to leave the house to vote.[27]

The Saturday night before the election, a local chapter of the Ku Klux Klan marched through the streets of the city to intimidate black voters. The klan chapter known as Stonewall Jackson No. 1 formed in a private space declaring that "no one discovers the meeting place of the order, the point of assembly or the place of disbandment." They also wore robes and hoods to draw parallels to the days of the original klan claiming "the same costumes that their ancestors wore in reconstruction [sic] days." They declared that their objective was to "fight to the death against the domination of the South or the United States by negroes or persons of foreign birth, regardless of their nationality." Dressed anonymously, the Klan marched through the streets of downtown Jacksonville, blasting horns to announce their arrival. They exhibited signs that read, "We were here yesterday! We are here today! We will be here forever!" Although there was no klan in Reconstruction era Jacksonville, the message of the sign was meant to express that white male supremacy had been around throughout that time and the klan now as then were the guardians of that movement.[28]

The Ku Klux Klan in Jacksonville had its origins in the success of the women's suffrage movement. In an envelope delivered to the offices of the *Florida Times-Union* the klan released its manifesto. They claimed that the klan was "determined that the traditions of the South and of pure Americanism shall be perpetuated." They claimed they advocated for "justice for all people . . . [the klan] stands against violence at all times, for cooperation with constituted legal authority for the purity of the ballot, for the sanctity of womanhood and the home . . . for white supremacy against all elements and bodies foreign or otherwise." Black women registering to vote represented to the Ku Klux Klan a disorder. They were acting in their minds as agents of the state or at least in accordance with the state to return not only the ballot to white male supremacy but also the home with their wives and daughters.[29]

Instead of being intimidated, black women appeared at the parade and jeered the klan as well as waited in lines as long as city blocks to vote the next day. According to coverage of the events, it is hard to know if black men too came to jeer at the klan: since black women had more latitude in racial transgressions because of their gender it is conceivable black men in large numbers did not turn out. The large number of black women lined up and down Bay Street to jeer, shout, call the klan participants names, and laugh at them. One report stated that a black woman shouted, "you ain't done nothing. Those German guns didn't scare us and we know white robes won't do it now." Although they knew they could no longer elect local officials, black voters hoped that they could have some influence in electing Warren G. Harding, a Republican, as president.

James Weldon Johnson, of the NAACP, feared violence in and around the election. In a letter to James Seth Hills he confessed that he thought the threat of white violence was a bluff, but if it were not he hoped that "colored men will back colored women up and stand together to defy the throng." He predicted that the "colored people of Jacksonville [would] keep their backbone stiff." Hills reported back to Johnson that the local NAACP organized thousands of blacks to come out to the parade to show unequivocally that they were not intimidated and in fact "ridiculed" the Ku Klux Klan publicly.[30]

When the results were counted, very few votes for Harding were cast in the predominately black districts. By this time, conservative Southern Democrats were discarding the black vote altogether and replacing votes for Republican candidates with Democratic candidates.[31] Walter F. White, of the NAACP, reported in the *New Republic* that thousands of African American men and women showed up to vote. Other African Americans provided food for those who stood in line to cast their ballot. James W. Floyd estimated that over two thousand black voters were turned away by white election officials at the polls and over sixteen thousand black voters never cast a ballot. Floyd compiled names and affidavits of victims of disfranchisement and submitted them to the national office of the NAACP. Johnson used this evidence to petition the U.S. Congress to investigate this and other cases of voter fraud throughout the South.[32]

Jacksonville's Democratic Party won the elections. According to the election results, barely any Republican votes were cast even within the majority black wards. White and the NAACP claimed the election was fraudulent. They tried to contest the results, but failed. However, Jacksonville's African Americans had scored a real victory: they had defied the Ku Klux Klan publicly and received national press attention. Blacks were not pushed out of the public sphere.[33]

The city's recent past had been marred by racial strife—including the first reported lynching just fourteen months earlier. What local residents were witnessing was black women openly engaging in the public sphere. The street, the sidewalks, and the public spaces were a stage where the citizenry performed political theatre. Most observers probably did not understand that this election, this parade, and the theatre attached to it was a single moment in a fifty-seven-year struggle for blacks to engage freely in the public sphere. Oftentimes, moments like this—where blacks engaged the public in critical ways—were usually met with a swift reaction. On Election Day the local papers reported that the police were issuing blank warrants "for the arrest of Negro men and women who had improperly registered, when they presented themselves for voting."[34] This back and forth had come to epitomize the history of the public sphere and public space for blacks throughout these five decades. As blacks pushed out into the public spaces of the city to engage in the public sphere, white lawmakers, municipal officers, and white private citizens then pushed blacks out of the public spaces to silence them. These actions represented a discourse between black and white residents.

Walter F. White was aware of this when he stated:

Unless the problem of the ballot is solved . . . our race riots and similar disturbances are just the beginning. This may sound pessimistic and as though the problem were viewed only from the standpoint of an alarmist. That is not the case. It is based upon the innermost feelings and thoughts of twelve million Americans who seek to be free.[35]

Following this White concluded:

The Negro emerged from slavery ignorant, uneducated, superstitious. It was a simple task to terrify him by sight of a band of men, clothed in white coming down a lonely road on a moonlight night.

Today, the Negro is neither so poor nor so ignorant nor so easily terrified, a fact known apparently to everybody but the revivers of the Ku Klux Klan.[36]

What White did not understand was that this theatre he witnessed was not the emergence of a "New Negro" or an aberration, but a single moment in a long history of the black counterpublic engaging the public sphere in the Urban South.

Epilogue

Making the Invisible Visible

One of Jacksonville's most prominent native sons, James Weldon Johnson, looked back with conflicted emotions over the evolution of his hometown in the years since he was a child. For him, the most important characteristic that caused him such pain was the way in which the city became strictly racialized. Johnson believed that white residents and lawmakers alike imposed a strict enforcement of Jim Crow on all political, economic, and social interactions. In his autobiography *Along This Way* he reflected on this:

> When I was growing up, most of the city policemen were Negroes; several members of the city council Negroes; one or two justices of the peace. . . . many of the best stalls in the city market were owned and operated by Negroes. . . . I know for a fact that Jacksonville was controlled by certain aristocratic families . . . who were sensitive to the code, *noblesse oblige*. The aristocratic families have lost control and the old conditions have been changed. Jacksonville is today a one hundred per cent Cracker town.[1]

Johnson's sanguine reflection promotes a familiar trope in that the mechanism of white supremacy in the South was a revolt of the white masses. The study of the public sphere and public space in Jacksonville complicates that narrative.

Throughout Jacksonville's history during this time the state, by way of federal troops or political machinations, imposed white political supremacy through legislation, constitutional conventions, judicial decisions, and private associations. White supremacy imposed throughout the public spaces of the city was a little difficult to maintain at all times. However, when blacks on the margin defied white supremacy, their actions could be interpreted as being "out of order," and thus their access to the public space could be restricted or policed. Although the aristocratic families may have had a sense of noblesse oblige when engaging with groups outside the center, the political white elite over time were just as interested in maintaining the structures of white supremacy as were poor and working-class whites.

The story of Jacksonville during this time is a history of a number of groups on the margin who move from the private to the public sphere with various degrees of success. As Mary P. Ryan has demonstrated in *Civic Wars*, the United States in the nineteenth century was a time when women, blacks, and workers came into public life as never before. Thus Jacksonville was not unique in this regard. What we learn from the evolution of the public sphere is that there is not a unitary public, but multiple publics, or as Nancy Fraser postulates subaltern counterpublics. While these publics are discursive, they do push and contest each other in the public and private spaces.[2]

The story of the color line and the public sphere in the South is best epitomized by the literary theme of invisibility. Ralph Ellison in *Invisible Man* opens the novel with the main character describing himself:

> I am an invisible man. . . . I am a man of substance, of flesh and bone, fiber and liquids—and I might even be said to posses a mind. I am invisible, understand, simply because people refuse to see me. . . . When they approach me they see only my surroundings, themselves, or figments of their imagination—indeed, everything and anything except me.[3]

The idea that the main character is invisible to white America is a metaphor for how whites engaged the color line. Racial segregation was to render blacks and their true selves "invisible" within a cultural geography. A consequence of that would be that their speech within the public sphere too would be silent if not invisible.

Since the 1980s, historians have tried to locate the origin of the African American civil rights movement. Originally Robert Korstad, Nelson Lichtenstein, and Aldon D. Morris mapped out the birth of the movement in the organizing of the 1940s. A decade later Robin D. G. Kelley and Michael K. Honey found that the road to Brown v. Board began with the Great Depression and New Deal era organizing by unions and the Communist Party. Since 2000, historians have tried to push back that origin to the 1910s and 1920s. The most important of this trend is Glenda Elizabeth Gilmore's *Defying Dixie,* which highlights the centrality of left-leaning organizations and movements from World War I in laying the groundwork for killing Jim Crow during the Cold War years.[4]

Gilmore argues that the radicals of the 1910s and 1920s were the catalyst for the modern civil rights movement as epitomized by the Brown decision. If valid, then the catalyst for that activism had its origin in the nineteenth century. The movement in Jacksonville in 1919 had its origin in the Reconstruction Era organizing of black troops mustered out of the army and questioning the meaning of black citizenship and the black women who protested in front of the Freedmen's Bureau office to demand federal officials force white employers to honor their contracts. If we imagine the civil rights movement as a discourse on black citizenship, as opposed to only actions and organizations, we can reconstruct a long history dating back to the antebellum abolitionists who took up the cause of Northern blacks' ability to attend white schools, sit with whites on public transportation, and seek legal protection from the court system.[5]

Although this history speaks to the African American past it also touches on contemporary issues of public space, citizenship, and civic engagement. Both Frederick Douglass and W.E.B. Du Bois drew the connections between Jim Crow and the plight of people of color throughout the world. Most twentieth-century historians have conceived of racial segregation through an exceptional framework located in time and space. Even though "right to the city" is not an exact experience to Jim Crow, as a function and process of controlling and embedding inequality with a subaltern class it shares many similarities. The fight against Jim Crow can also inform us as to the pernicious policies the state enforces to reclaim public space to limit speech whether it be for the homeless in Los Angeles, the favelas of São Paulo, or the Occupy Movement that captured Wall Street and numerous U.S. cities in 2011.

What does this tell us about the subaltern and the public sphere? It reveals that the public sphere is not a location of unitary consensus but of tension, where the dominant public tries to render the subaltern invisible and the subaltern counterpublic pushes into the public sphere for visibility. This explains the story of women both during the French Revolution and in nineteenth-century America who tried to push themselves out into the public sphere. As well as the gay and lesbian counterpublic exemplified by the closet and what it meant to be out of the closet and part of public life after the 1960s. And also to be the poor and disfranchised in the Global South who live far outside the cities in shantytowns and favelas—invisible to residents in the city center. At long last, blacks in the Jim Crow South refused to be invisible residents in the public sphere.

Notes

Introduction

1. Du Bois, *Souls*, 64, 142; Douglass, "The Color Line," 567–77.

2. Woodward, *Strange Career*, xi–xiii; Ayers, *Promise of the New South*, 143–46; Rabinowitz, *Race Relations*, xxi–xxiv.

3. Du Bois, *Souls*, 2–35; Du Bois, *Black Reconstruction*, 711–29.

4. Crewdson, "Invisibility," 1–16.

5. Habermas, *Structural Transformation*, 25–43.

6. Landes, *Women and the Public Sphere*, 169–200; Ryan, *Women in Public*, 172–80; Fraser, "Rethinking the Public Sphere," 109–42. Michael Warner uses this paradigm of counterpublics to examine the gay and lesbian public sphere in *Publics and Counterpublics*.

7. Asen and Brouwer, eds., *Counterpublics and the State*, 8–9; Higginbotham, *Righteous Discontent*, 7–9; Dawson, *Black Visions*, 23–27.

8. Blair L. M. Kelley, *Right to Ride*, 11–14. See also Whaley, *Disciplining Women*, 3–12.

9. Lefebvre, *Production of Space*, 244–45; Harvey, *Justice, Nature, and the Geography of Difference*, 110; Sewell, *Women and the Everyday City*, 120.

10. Cresswell, *In Place/Out of Place*, 22–23; Mike Davis, "Fortress Los Angeles," 154–80.

11. Robin D. G. Kelley, "We Are Not What We Seem," 75–112; Ortiz, *Emancipation Betrayed*, 229–36.

12. Keller, *Triumph of Order*, 203–14.

13. Lopes de Souza, "Cities for People," 483–92; Mayer, "The Right to the City," 362–74; Holston, *Insurgent Citizenship*, 3–38.

14. See for example, Lassiter and Crespino, eds., *The Myth of Southern Exceptionalism*, 3–22; Bender, ed. *Rethinking American History*.

Chapter 1. Re-Ordered Spaces

1. Habermas, *Structural Transformation*, 25–43. See also Fraser, "Rethinking the Public Sphere," 109–42; Crawford, "Contesting the Public Realm," 4–9.

2. Camp, "I Could Not Stay There," 1–20; Camp, *Closer to Freedom*, 12–34.

3. *Florida Union*, 27 May 1865.

4. Schwartz, ed., *A Woman Doctor's Civil War*, 176–77.

5. *Zion's Herald and Wesleyan Journal*, 15 June 1864. See also Foner, *Reconstruction*, 77–101.

6. *Liberator*, 15 April 1864. See also Joe M. Richardson, "We Are Truly Doing Missionary Work," 185; Schwartz ed., *A Woman Doctor's Civil War*, 175–76.

7. *Christian Recorder*, 14 January 1865.

8. Ibid., 18 September 1864.

9. Soldiers with the U.S.C.T. stationed in Jacksonville frequently mentioned their lack of pay as well as their being denied promotion in letters to the *Christian Recorder* in the Spring of 1864 (16 April 1864; 7 and 28 May 1864). One solider claimed to have deserted the army when he realized he could not be promoted to an officer because of his race. (General Court-Martial Records, Transcript of General Court-Martial of Pvt. Joseph Barranger, LL1880.)

10. *Christian Recorder*, 16 April 1864.

11. Ibid., 7 May 1864.

12. Ibid.

13. General Court-Martial Records, Transcript of General Court-Martial of Assistant Surgeon John V. DeGrasse, NN2809; Transcript of General Court-Martial of Capt. Henry McIntire, NN2943; and Transcript of General Court-Martial of Capt. Henry M. Jordan, MM 3322.

14. General Court-Martial Records, Transcript of General Court-Martial of 2nd Lt. Henry K. Cady, MM3322.

15. Bennett, "The Jacksonville Mutiny," 39.

16. Ibid., 42.

17. General Court-Martial Records, Transcript of General Court-Martial of Charles A. Merritt, NN2479; Transcript of General Court-Martial of John Q. Adams, LL2294; Transcript of General Court-Martial of Thomas Wright, LL2811.

18. General Court-Martial Records, Transcript of General Court-Martial of Charles Sewell, OO566. Also see *New York Times*, 2 March 1864; Schwartz, ed., *A Woman Doctor's Civil War*, 61.

19. General Court-Martial Records, Transcript of General Court-Martial of Samuel Johnson, MM3122; Transcript of General Court-Martial of Henry K. Cady, MM3322.

20. General Court-Martial Records, Transcript of General Court-Martial of Jacob Plowder, Joseph Nathaniel, James Allen, and Richard Lee, OO1477. Also see Fannin, "The Jacksonville Mutiny," 388–94.

21. Eveleth quoted in Joe M. Richardson, "We Are Truly Doing Missionary Work," 185–86.

22. *Zion's Herald and Wesleyan Journal*, 4 May 1864.

23. Ibid.

24. Ibid., 15 June 1864.

25. *Liberator*, 15 April 1864; *New York Times*, 27 December 1865, 11 June 1866; *Christian Recorder*, 16 May 1868.

26. *Christian Advocate*, 12 June 1873, 23 July 1874, 4 March 1880; *Zion's Herald and Wesleyan Journal*, 17 February 1876; *Florida Times-Union*, 25 April 1884, 29 April 1887.

27. *New York Observer and Chronicle*, 14 May 1874; *Zion's Herald and Wesleyan Journal*, 17 February 1876; *Christian Advocate*, 4 March 1880. See also Russell, *Life and Labors*, 25–26; City of Jacksonville, Jacksonville City Directory, 1870–1920, 9; American Missionary Association Archives, February 1870 Stanton Report, Manuscript [1970] reel 28; Cookman Institute of Jacksonville, Florida, *Catalogue of Cookman Institute, 1886–1887*, Central Florida Memory Project, accessed 2 September 2011, http://www.cfmemory.org.

28. *Florida Times-Union*, 7 April 1876, 20 March 1884, and *New York Age*, 11 April 1885.

29. Schwartz, ed., *A Woman Doctor's Civil War*, 235–36; *Tallahassee Floridian*, 16 February 1866.

30. *Jacksonville Herald*, 24 August 1865.

31. *Liberator*, 25 August 1865, 8 September 1865, and 6 October 1865.

32. Ibid., 1 September 1865.

33. Ibid., 20 October 1865.

34. Ibid., 1 September 1865. See also State of Florida, *Acts and Resolutions* (1866), 25.

Chapter 2. Democratized Space

1. *Florida Union*, 1 July 1865, 7 October 1865.

2. Ibid., 14 October 1865; *Jacksonville Herald*, 22 September 1865.

3. Shofner, *Nor Is It Over Yet*, 39–42; State of Florida, Constitution (1865), art. VI, § 1; *Florida Union*, 4 November 1865, and *Florida Times*, 5 October 1865.

4. *Florida Times*, 5 October 1865.

5. Shofner, *Nor Is It Over Yet*, 39–40; State of Florida, Constitution (1865), art. I, § 8; *Florida Times-Union*, 25 January 1866.

6. State of Florida, Constitution (1865), art. I, § 8; *Florida Times-Union*, 25 January 1866.

7. Shofner, *Nor Is It Over Yet*, 158–59; *Florida Union*, 1 June 1867.

8. *Florida Union*, 1 June 1867.

9. Ibid.

10. Ibid.

11. Union Republican Club of Jacksonville, Proceedings [1867], Florida Historical Society.

12. *Florida Union*, 5 October 1867; J. M. Fairbanks to J. P. Bouse, 10 November 1867, Edward M. L'Engle Papers, Southern Historical Collection; C. Thurston Chase to George Whipple, 11 May 1868, American Missionary Association Archives, Manuscript [1970]

reel 28; State of Florida, Constitution (1868), "Declaration of Rights," § 1, 14, art. IV, § 27; *Florida Union*, 16 May 1868; Cox, "Military Reconstruction in Florida," 219–33.

13. State of Florida, Constitution (1868), art. XVI, § XXVIII; State of Florida, *Acts and Resolutions* (1870), 35 and (1873), 25–26.

14. Perman, *The Road to Redemption*, 264–365.

15. *Florida Union*, 23 December 1868.

16. Frederick T. Davis, *History of Jacksonville*, 294–97; *Tallahassee Sentinel*, 9 April 1870, and *Tallahassee Weekly Floridian*, 12 April 1870.

17. Robert C. Lowry to Frank Howard, and Robert C. Lowry to M.H.G. Sandens, 15 May 1867, Bureau of Refugees, Freedmen, and Abandoned Lands, Record Group M1869, NARA [Microfilm], roll 14.

18. Andrew Mahoney, "Monthly Report Freedman's Offices March 31, June 1, July 1, 1867," Bureau of Refugees, Freedman, and Abandoned Lands, Record Group M1869, NARA [Microfilm], roll 8.

19. Ibid., "January 18th, 1867."

20. Cox, "Military Reconstruction in Florida," 219–33.

21. Shofner, *Nor Is It Over Yet*, 264–69; Frederick T. Davis, *History of Jacksonville*, 150–52.

22. *Newark Daily Advertiser*, 1 March 1869.

23. C. C. Gilbert to Edward Hopkins, 24 February 1869, and E. A. Coolidge to Charles C. Raven, 26 February 1869, Records of the United States Army Continental Commands, 1821–1920, Record Group 393.

24. Ibid.

25. *Mercury and Floridian*, 27 February 1869; Frederick T. Davis, *History of Jacksonville*, 151–52.

26. *Tallahassee Weekly Floridian*, 2 March 1869.

27. *Newark Daily Advertiser*, 1 March 1869.

28. C. C. Gilbert to Assistant Adjutant General, 26 February 1869, Records of the United States Army Continental Commands, 1821–1920, Record Group 393.

29. *Tallahassee Weekly Floridian*, 2 March 1869.

30. C. C. Gilbert to Assistant Adjutant General, 26 February 1869, Records of the United States Army Continental Commands, 1821–1920, Record Group 393; *St. Augustine Examiner*, 30 March 1869.

Chapter 3. The Mob-Public

1. For the idea of the "mob-public" see Bakhtin, *Rabelais and His World*; Lennard J. Davis, "The Social Construction of Public Locations," 23–40.

2. On the meeting of high and low culture during festivals see Stallybrass and White, *The Politics of Poetics*, 1–27.

3. According to Edward C. Williamson, these "independents" would have been outside of the Bourbon Democrats and been critical of big business and railroads much like the populists who emerge throughout this era. Since campaign literature and speeches have not survived during these two elections it is hard to tell equivocally if these local independents were part of the statewide independent movement since Northern white

Democrats would have shared similar economic policies with the Bourbons during this time rather than the independents.

4. Frederick T. Davis, *History of Jacksonville*, 296–97; *Florida Times-Union*, 1 and 4 April 1876; City of Jacksonville, Jacksonville City Directory (1876–1877), 57. For "Independentism," see Edward C. Williamson, *Florida Politics*.

5. *Florida Union*, 8 March 1876.

6. *Christian Recorder*, 31 May 1877.

7. Akin, "When a Minority Becomes the Majority," 123–25; Barbara Ann Richardson, "History of Blacks in Jacksonville," 196–97; *Florida Union*, 11 March 1877, 12 November 1878, 8 November 1882, and *Daily Florida Standard*, 22 March 1882, 7 February 1884, 18 March 1884. In Florida during Reconstruction, African Americans could not by law represent the state of Florida in the U.S. Congress, as lieutenant governor or governor unless they were a citizen of the state for more than nine years and a registered voter. In addition, the way voting districts were divided by the legislature put large African Americans communities at a disadvantage in electing state and national representation. Joe M. Richardson, *Negro in the Reconstruction*, 158.

8. State of Florida, Constitution (1885), art. VI, § 8 and art. VIII, § 5; Edward C. Williamson, "The Constitutional Convention," 116–26; *Journal of the Proceedings of the Constitutional Convention*, 9, 361, 402–3; *New York Globe*, 26 January 1884, 16 February 1884.

9. Perman, *Struggle for Mastery*, 321–28.

10. *New York Freeman*, 12 September 1885.

11. State of Florida, Constitution (1885), art. V, § 8, 15; *New York Freeman*, 12 September 1885.

12. *Florida Times-Union*, 4 October 1885.

13. State of Florida, Constitution (1885), art. VI, § 8 and art. VIII, § 5; Edward C. Williamson, "The Constitutional Convention," 116–26; *Journal of the Proceedings of the Constitutional Convention*, 361, 402–3.

14. *Journal of the Proceedings of the Constitutional Convention*, 311, 316; *Florida Times-Union*, 22 and 23 February 1886.

15. *Florida Times-Union*, 26 March 1887, 5 April 1887.

16. Ibid.

17. Ibid., 26 and 30 March 1887, 5 April 1887.

18. Ibid., 12 April 1887.

19. *New York Freeman*, 23 July 1887; *Florida Times-Union*, 6 and 12 April 1887.

20. *Florida Times-Union*, 26 and 27 June 1887.

21. Ibid., 6, 8, and 14 December 1887, 5 and 31 March 1888, 17 April 1888; Smith v. Burbridge, 24 Fla. 112, 3 So., 869 (1888).

22. Smith *v.* Burbridge; Fairlie, "The Yellow Fever Epidemic," 95–108; *Florida Times-Union*, 7 November 1888.

23. *New York Age*, 8 November 1888, 1 December 1888.

24. Fairlie, "The Yellow Fever Epidemic," 95–108; *Florida Times-Union*, 7 November 1888, 22 April 1892.

25. *Florida Times-Union*, 22 February 1889, 10 and 11 April 1889; Gilmore, *Gender and Jim Crow*, 96–97.

26. While the local press was unclear why they were called dirty shirters, it was probably some play on the late nineteenth century saying, "waving the red shirt." Civil War veterans who ran for political office would wave a bloodied shirt at speeches as a symbol of what they sacrificed for the country. These dirty shirters probably waved a "dirty shirt" as a sign that they were pushed down to the ground and their clothing was soiled by blacks in the city.

27. *Florida Times-Union*, 22 February 1889, 10 and 11 April 1889.

28. Ibid., 12, 13, 16, and 20 April 1889.

29. Ibid.

30. Ibid., 18 April 1889; *New York Age*, 1 December 1888, 20 April 1889. Fortune and his brother claimed that Douglass was putting on a show during this time to white audiences to secure a federal appointment with the incoming Benjamin Harrison administration.

31. Ibid., 17 April 1889.

32. Ibid., 20 and 21 April 1889, 3, 10, 14, 17, and 22 May 1889.

33. *New York Age*, 25 May 1889, 1 June 1889.

34. Ibid., 1 June 1889.

35. *Daily Florida Standard*, 4 October 1890, 11 November 1890, and *Florida Times-Union*, 4 and 8 November 1890.

36. *Florida Times-Union*, 29 December 1890.

37. Ibid., 22 April 1892.

38. Ibid., 1, 19, and 20 May 1892.

39. Ibid, 24 April 1892, 20 May 1892.

40. Ibid., 18, 19, 20, 22, and 23 July 1893, and *Evening Telegram*, 2, 3, 6, and 8 May 1893; Johnson, *Along This Way*, 140–41.

41. At least two black councilmen represented Jacksonville's predominately black sixth ward between 1893 and 1907.

42. *Florida Times-Union*, 18, 19, 20, 22, and 23 July 1893, and *Evening Telegram*, 2, 3, 6, and 8 July 1893.

43. Ibid., 11, 13, 18, 19, 20, and 21 June 1895; Goodwin, "Joseph E. Lee of Jacksonville," 1–80.

Chapter 4. The Black Counterpublic Emerges

1. Fraser, "Rethinking the Public Sphere," 109–42.

2. *Liberator*, 1 September 1865.

3. *Florida Union*, 3 April 1876.

4. Ibid., 27 and 28 February 1890; Johnson, *Along This Way*, 131.

5. *Florida Times-Union*, 27 and 28 February 1890.

6. Ibid., 5 July 1892.

7. Ibid.

8. Johnson in his book *Along This Way* gives some details into the planning of this event and the involvement of both Jones and Tresvan. However, he seems to have conflated the Lowe death with that of Burrows as one and the same incident. More than likely it would indicate that Jones was inspired by the plan when Armstrong was arrested for the death of Officer Lowe and had prepared for this over the next two years.

9. *Florida Times-Union*, 6, 8, and 9 July 1892; *North American*, 7 July 1892; *New York Times*, 7 July 1892. Johnson, *Along This Way*, 131–32. See also Ortiz, *Emancipation Betrayed*, 183–86.

10. *New York Age*, 9 March 1889.

11. Ibid.; *Florida Times-Union*, 18 December 1886, 16 February 1889.

12. *Florida Times-Union*, 6 and 7 July 1892, and *New York Times*, 7 July 1892; Johnson, *Along This Way*, 132.

13. *Florida Times-Union*, 7 July 1892.

14. Ibid.

15. Ibid., 8 July 1892; Johnson, *Along This Way*, 132.

16. *New York Times*, 8 December 1895.

17. Ortiz, *Emancipation Betrayed*, 76–81.

18. *Florida Times-Union*, 30 November 1900, 30 March 1901; Wilbanks, *Forgotten Heroes*, 30.

19. *New York Times*, 12 August 1897.

Chapter 5. Representations of Private Spaces

1. Lefebvre, *Production of Space*, 33, 41–49; Harvey, *Justice, Nature, and the Geography of Difference*, 112, 230.

2. Rabinowitz, *Race Relations*, 202–3.

3. State of Florida, *Acts and Resolutions* (1881), 85–86; State of Florida, Constitution (1885) art. XVI, § 24. *New York Age*, 12 September 1885. Black men marrying white women was considered a misdemeanor, while white men who married a woman at least one-eighth black were charged with a felony that could include prosecuting any county clerk, judge, or pastor knowingly assisting in such ceremonies with a fine or jail time. Antebellum Florida laws punished white men more severely than black men for miscegenation due to the fact that white men were expected to embody moral standards through example. See Robinson, *Dangerous Liaisons*, 9–10.4. *Florida Times Union*, 8 March 1876.

5. *Zion's Herald and Wesleyan Journal*, 30 December 1875.

6. Ibid., 17 February 1876.

7. *New York Evangelist*, 3 January 1884; *Christian Index*, 9 November 1882; *Zion's Herald and Wesleyan Journal*, 24 February 1876; *Christian Advocate*, 2 June 1881.

8. *Zion's Herald and Wesleyan Journal*, 24 February 1876.

9. *Christian Advocate*, 2 June 1881.

10. Ibid., 2 June 1881, 28 July 1881, 25 August 1881.

11. Ibid., 25 January 1883; *Zion's Herald and Wesleyan Journal*, 8 February 1888.

12. *Christian Advocate*, 12 June 1873, 23 July 1874, 4 March 1880; *Zion's Herald and Wesleyan Journal*, 17 February 1876; *Florida Times-Union*, 25 April 1884, 29 April 1887.

13. *New York Observer and Chronicle*, 14 May 1874; *Zion's Herald and Wesleyan Journal*, 17 February 1876; *Christian Advocate*, 4 March 1880. Russell, *Life and Labors*, 25–26; City of Jacksonville, Jacksonville City Directory (1870), 9; American Missionary Association Archives, February 1870 Stanton Report, 28 Manuscript [1970] reel 28; Cookman

Institute of Jacksonville, Florida, *Catalogue of Cookman Institute, 1886–1887*, Central Florida Memory Project, accessed 2 September 2011, http://www.cfmemory.org.

14. *Western Christian Advocate*, 29 August 1883; *Christian Advocate*, 4 August 1887; *Zion's Herald and Wesleyan Journal*, 16 March 1898, 5 November 1902. More than likely, other black schools served nonblack populations of color within the city as the Boylan Home did; however, evidence of this is not as forthcoming.

15. *Zion's Herald and Wesleyan Journal*, 30 December 1875.

16. Ibid., 30 December 1875, 30 March 1876; *Christian Standard*, 16 April 1881.

17. *Florida Times-Union*, 7 April 1876, 20 March 1884, and *New York Age*, 11 April 1885.

18. *American Missionary* 38 (November 1884): 332; *American Missionary* 46 (April 1892): 125.

19. Ibid., 50 (July 1896): 215–17.

20. *Independent*, 4 August 1892, 2 November 1893.

21. Ibid., 4 August 1892.

22. Ibid., 2 November 1893.

23. Ibid.

24. Ibid.

25. Florida Department of Education, "Biennial Report of the Superintendent of Instruction" (1890), 6–7 and "Biennial Report of the Superintendent of Instruction," (1894), 69.

26. *Independent*, 15 August 1895, and *Florida Times-Union*, 5 September 1895; State of Florida, *Acts and Resolutions* "Chapter 4335 [No. 14]" (*1895)*, 96–97. See also Joe M. Richardson "The Nest of Vile Fanatics," 399.

27. Florida Department of Education, "Biennial Report of the Superintendent of Instruction" (1895), 24.

28. *Florida Times-Union*, 5 October 1895.

29.Ibid.

30.Ibid., 5 September 1895, 5 October 1895; Florida Department of Education, "Biennial Report of the Superintendent of Instruction" (1897), 52–53.

31. *Outlook*, 17 and 31 August 1895, and *Independent*, 29 October 1896.

32. *American Missionary* 49 (September 1895): 286–88; *American Missionary* 49 (November 1895): 346; and *American Missionary* 49 (December 1895): 379–80.

33. *Liberty*, 11 January 1896; *American Missionary* 50 (May 1896): 146–47; *American Missionary* 50 (June 1896): 179–81; *Independent*, 16 April 1896.

34. *New York Times*, 23 October 1896; *Outlook*, 7 November 1896; *Congregationalist*, 30 April 1896. Florida Department of Education, "Biennial Report of the Superintendent of Instruction" (1897), 187–88.

35. State of Florida, *Digest of the School Laws*, 87; *Independent*, 30 October 1913.

Chapter 6. Representations of Public Spaces

1. *Christian Advocate*, 13 March 1873.

2. Payne, *Recollections of Seventy Years*, 281–88; *Savannah Morning News*, 13 August 1881.

3. Payne, *Recollections of Seventy Years*, 11, 286; *Christian Recorder*, 10 August 1882.

4. *Christian Recorder,* 13 April 1882.

5. Payne, *Recollections of Seventy Years,* 286–87.

6. Ibid., 287–88.

7. *Christian Recorder,* 3 August 1882.

8. Payne, *Recollections of Seventy Years,* 285–87; *Christian Recorder,* 27 April 1882, 3 August 1882.

9. Payne, *Recollections of Seventy Years,* 285–87; *Christian Recorder,* 27 April 1882, 3 August 1882.

10. *Christian Recorder,* 3 August 1882.

11. Ibid.

12. Ibid., 20 April 1882.

13. Ibid., 13 and 27 April 1882; Civil Rights Cases, 109 U.S. 3 (1883).

14. *Huntsville Gazette,* 29 April 1882; *Christian Recorder,* 3 August 1882; *Weekly Pelican,* 1 January 1887.

15. *Huntsville Gazette,* 29 April 1882.

16. Hunter, *To 'Joy My Freedom,* 115–16.

17. Gaines, *Uplifting the Race,* 31–32.

18. Ibid.

19. Williams v. Jacksonville, Tampa, and Key West Railroad, 26 Fla. 533, 8 So. 446 (1890).

20. Ibid.; Welke, "When All the Women Were White," 261–316. As for notions of Victorian era sexuality see Mumford, "'Lost Manhood' Found," 33–57 and Seidman, "The Power of Desire," 47–67.

21. *Florida Times-Union,* 24 February 1886.

22. State of Florida, *Laws of Florida 1887,* 116.

23. Ibid.

24. State of Florida, *Acts and Resolutions* (1890–1891), 114–15.

25. State of Florida, *Laws of Florida 1887,* 116; *Florida Times-Union,* 23 May 1887, 4 August 1895. See also Welke, "When All the Women Were White," 274.

26. The application of the term "Jim Crow" to separate accommodations goes back to the 1840s when abolitionists noticed that white passengers in the North demanded separate cars for free black passengers. Reporters in the *Liberator* used the term to denote not only the separate car, but also the racial insult and second-class status that this policy promoted. See *Liberator,* 5 November 1841, 28 April 1843, 1 August 1845; and Litwack, *North of Slavery,* 106–7.

27. *New York Freeman,* 23 July 1887.

28. *Florida Metropolis,* 18 June 1901, and *Florida Times-Union,* 18 June 1901.

29. *Florida Metropolis,* 6 November 1901, and *Florida Times-Union,* 6 November 1901.

30. *Florida Metropolis,* 8 November 1901. For similar incidents in World War II–era Birmingham, see Robin D. G. Kelley, *Race Rebels,* 63.

31. This was the father of James Weldon Johnson, future secretary of the NAACP. At this time the younger Johnson was living in New York with his brother Rosemond. Later in life when he wrote his autobiography *Along This Way,* he recalls traveling back and

forth to Jacksonville in 1901. However, James Weldon Johnson does not mention this protest or his father's role in these activities.

32. *Florida Metropolis,* 8 November 1901.

33. Ibid., 9 November 1901.

34. Ibid., 11 November 1901.

35. Ibid.; *Florida Times–Union,* 11 November 1901, and *Atlanta Constitution,* 11 November 1901.

36. *Cleveland Gazette,* 12 April 1902; *Savannah Tribune,* 16 and 23 November 1901; *Colored American,* 30 November 1901; *Indianapolis Freeman,* 30 November 1901.

37. *Wichita Search,* 23 November 1901; *Savannah Tribune,* 23 November 1901; *Indianapolis Freeman,* 7 December 1901; *Florida Times–Union,* 20 July 1905.

38. Gross Earnings of the Main Street Railroad Company 1900–1902, Box 38, Southern Historical Collection; M. E. Satchwell to George Baldwin, 25 February 1902, in George Johnson Baldwin Papers (hereafter cited as Baldwin Papers), Southern Historical Collection. The North Jacksonville Line would remain in black hands until 1903, and then two white owners took it over and continued to hire black employees while desperately trying to sell the company to investors in New Jersey. Throughout this time they advertised this as the "black" owned streetcar, even though most black residents knew otherwise.

39. Baldwin to Stone and Webster, 5 March 1903, Box 39; Baldwin to Stone and Webster, 10 April 1903, Box 39; Wetmore to William W. Osborne, 10 April 1903, Box 39; Tucker to Baldwin, 21 October 1904 and 31 December 1904. Baldwin Papers, Box 40, Southern Historical Collection.

40. Everywhere else in the South that enforced segregation ordinances required separate compartments, and signs denoting black and white patrons had to be visible and strictly enforced.

41. Tucker to Baldwin, 31 December 1904 and 28 January 1905, Baldwin Papers, Box 40, Southern Historical Collection.

42. Ibid.

43. *Florida Times-Union,* 6 June 1905.

44. *Pensacola Journal,* 26 and 30 April 1905.

45. *Pensacola Journal,* 14, 15, 18, 19, 26, and 30 April 1905.

46. Knight to Baldwin, 17 April 1905; Knight to Baldwin, 24 April 1905; and Baldwin to Knight, 24 April 1905. Baldwin Papers, Box 55, Southern Historical Collection.

47. Baldwin to Stone and Webster, 6 June 1905 and General Notice to Motormen and Conductors, 30 June 1905, Baldwin Papers, Box 41, Southern Historical Collection.

48. Resolutions in Condemnation of the Iniquitous "Jim Crow" Streetcar Law, 12 June 1905, Box 41; Baldwin to Stone and Webster, 17 July 1905, Box 55; Baldwin to Tucker, 7 June 1905, Box 41. Baldwin Papers, Southern Historical Collection. See also *Pensacola Journal,* 14 May 1905, 25 July 1905, and *Afro American Ledger,* 15 July 1905.

49. Resolutions in Condemnation of the Iniquitous "Jim Crow" Streetcar Law, 12 June 1905, Baldwin Papers, Box 41, Southern Historical Collection.

50. Wetmore to Baldwin, 23 June 1905 and Baldwin to Stone and Webster, 7 July 1905,

Baldwin Papers, Box 41, Southern Historical Collection; *New York Age,* 20 July 1905. In coverage of the boycott in the black press, Waldron and Wetmore are reported to be in cooperation. According to the letters to Baldwin from Wetmore, Wetmore seems as if he is not enchanted by Waldron and wants to earnestly help to avoid a boycott and claims Waldron is out for political influence and self-promotion. Wetmore mentions in his letters that he would be attacked if people knew the relationship that he and Baldwin had for the previous year.

51. Baldwin to Stone and Webster, 12 July 1905; Wetmore to Baldwin, 14 June 1905; Wetmore to Baldwin, 9 June 1905; Stone and Webster to Baldwin, 14 June 1905; Baldwin to J. E. Hartridge, 6 June 1905; and Wetmore to Baldwin, 8 June 1905. Baldwin Papers, Box 41, Southern Historical Collection.

52. *Florida Times-Union,* 20 July 1905; *Florida Metropolis,* 20 July 1905; *Washington Bee,* 29 July 1905, 12 August 1905; *Afro American Ledger,* 29 July 1905, 5 and 12 August 1905; *Pensacola Journal,* 25 July 1905; *New York Age,* 20 and 27 July 1905.

53. Florida Supreme Court, "Purcell v. State: Introductory Statement and Result of Suit," "Opinion: Judgment Affirmed," (June Term 1905) and Florida v. Andrew Patterson, Florida Reports 50 (1905), 126–27; *Florida Times-Union,* 21, 23, 25, 26, and 30 July 1905.

54. Florida Supreme Court, "Purcell v. State: Introductory Statement of Nature and Result of Suit" (June Term 1905) and Florida v. Patterson, 50 Fla. 127, 39 So. 398 (1905).

55. There is also an element of skin color that plays a role. The black newspapers identify Wetmore as a man of light complexion. They conclude that because of this he could have passed for white, but choose to identify himself as black. The papers believed he was brave and heroic for this decision.

56. City of Jacksonville, Jacksonville City Council Minutes, 17 October 1905, 501–2; *Florida Times-Union,* 18 October 1905; Pensacola, City Council Minutes, 27 September 1905; *Florida Times-Union,* 7 and 8 September 1906. See also Tucker to Baldwin, 13 November 1905 and Wetmore to Baldwin, 13 November 1905, Baldwin Papers, Box 41, Southern Historical Collection. And see Crooms v. Schad, 51 Fla. 168, 40 So. 497 and Patterson v. Taylor, 51 Fla. 275, 40 So. 493 (1906); *New York Age,* 10 August 1905; State of Florida, *Acts and Resolutions* (1915), 99–101; Florida East Coast Railroad Company v. Geiger, 64 Fla., 60 So. 753.

57. Wetmore to Baldwin, 26 June 1905 and Wetmore to Baldwin, 15 November 1905, Baldwin Papers, Box 41, Southern Historical Collection.

58. It is hard to tell whether the boycott truly ended after this compromise. Since the reporters were on the payroll they may not have reported a continuing boycott. There was no coverage of any future boycotts in Jacksonville in the black press nationally; since the earlier ones were covered one would have to assume that both Waldron and Wetmore supporters agreed to the terms of the compromise. There is no indication of any boycott in the rest of Baldwin's papers. The story of Wetmore's suicide is mentioned in James Weldon Johnson's autobiography *Along This Way* (Wetmore is the frequently mentioned childhood friend "D").

59. *Florida Metropolis,* 6 April 1907. The voting stations in the first and sixth wards were across the street from each other thus making it easy for whites to vote, while making it difficult for African Americans to vote.

60. Ibid., 19 June 1907.

61. *Florida Times-Union*, 2 May 1907, and *Florida Metropolis*, 20 and 23 May 1907, 19 and 20 June 1907.

62. City of Jacksonville, *Charter and Ordinances* (1917), 280; Woodward, *Strange Career*, 116.

Chapter 7. Labor's Counterpublic

1. Ryan, *Civic Wars*, 183–227. See also Fraser, "Rethinking the Public Sphere," 109–42.

2. Herod, *Labor Geographies*, 13–49; Jepson, "Spaces of Labor Activism," 679–702.

3. *Tallahassee Weekly Floridian*, 27 May 1873, 3 June 1873.

4. Ibid., 10 June 1873.

5. Ibid.

6. Ibid.

7. *Savannah Morning News*, 27 June 1873.

8. Herod, *Labor Geographies*, 13–49; *Christian Advocate*, 13 June 1872; "Workingmen's Associations," 430; "The Co-Operative Movement," 131. See also City of Jacksonville, Jacksonville City Directory (1878–1879), 183 and Jacksonville City Directory (1886), 274c.

9. *Zion's Herald and Wesleyan Journal*, 20 May 1880.

10. *Savannah Morning News*, 22 and 23 June 1880.

11. Ibid., 28 and 29 June 1880

12. Ibid.

13. Ibid.

14. *Savannah Morning News*, 29, and 30 June 1880, and *Fernandina Florida Mirror*, 3 July 1880. On Kearneyites and Kearneyism see *Independent*, 4 July 1878. The local political issues that might have motivated black workers and white workers to organize are lost due to the Jacksonville newspapers not surviving from this era. Consult Edward C. Williamson, "Black Belt Political Crisis," 402–9.

15. The Jacksonville Light Infantry had its origin in protecting the city from Union occupation and was disbanded with the Confederate Army's surrender in 1865, while the First Florida Light Infantry was formed in 1877. As the city would grow, more militia units would form to assist in "protecting the peace." On the formation of the local and state militias see *Webb's Florida: Historical and Industrial Biography*, 124; Frederick T. Davis, *History of Jacksonville*, 461.

16. United Brotherhood of Carpenters and Joiners of America, "List of Local Unions," *Official Handbook* (1892), 1305; "Trade Notes," *Carpenter* 19 (August 1899): 1.

17. In St. Augustine only Henry M. Flagler held onto the ten hour workday while the rest of the city recognized the eight hour day. See "Trade Notes," *Carpenter* 20 (October 1900): 1; "Trade Notes," *Carpenter* 22 (February 1902): 2; "Victory for Tampa Union," *Carpenter* 22 (May 1902): 5.

18. *Florida Metropolis*, 18 July 1902.

19. *Florida Times-Union*, 19 July 1902, and *Florida Metropolis*, 19 July 1902; "The Situation in Jacksonville," *Carpenter* 22 (June 1902): 3.

20. *Florida Times-Union*, 23 July 1902, and *Florida Metropolis*, 22 and 23 July 1902.

21. *Florida Metropolis*, 23 July 1902.

22. Ibid.

23. On the use of strikebreakers as rioters see Norwood, *Strikebreaking and Intimidation*, 1–14.

24. *Florida Metropolis*, 24 and 25 July 1902 and 1 and 2 August 1902; *Florida Times-Union*, 25, 26, and 29 July 1902 and 2 August 1902.

25. *Florida Metropolis*, 5 and 7 August 1902, and *Florida Times-Union*, 8 August 1902.

26. *Florida Metropolis*, 5, 11, and 16 November 1912, and *Florida Times-Union*, 5 November 1912.

27. *Dixie*, 16 and 23 November 1912; *Florida Metropolis*, 5, 11, and 16 November 1912; *Florida Times-Union*, 5 November 1912. Also Baldwin to Henry G. Bradlee, 13 November 1912; H. H. Hunt to Baldwin, 14 January 1913; and "Annual Report to Directors of Jacksonville Traction Company" 1913—all in Baldwin Papers, Box 42, Southern Historical Collection.

28. *Florida Times-Union*, 27 July 1916; Railroad Commission of the State of Florida, "Annual Report of the Seaboard Air Line Railway Company," 31 December 1916, 510–11.

29. *Florida Metropolis*, 29 July 1916.

30. *Artisan*, 1 January 1916, 19 February 1916, 22 and 29 July 1916, 5 August 1916, 4 August 1917.

31. *Black Workers* [Microfilm], reel 11, frame 671.

32. Ibid., frame 664–71. Black women in Jacksonville utilized other venues for highlighting gender inequality like suffrage campaigns, where white women placed gender issues in the forefront of their labor campaigns (see Boris, "From Gender to Racialized Gender," 9–13).

33. See Arnesen, "Like Banquo's Ghost," 1601–33.

34. *Black Workers* [Microfilm], reel 10, frame 476–508.

35. Arnesen, *Brotherhoods of Color*, 42–83.

Chapter 8. Women's Counterpublic

1. Ayers, *Promise of the New South*, 132–59, 318–19; Brown, "To Catch the Vision of Freedom" in Ann D. Gordon et al., eds., *African American Women and the Vote*, 66–99; *Florida Times-Union*, 7 November 1888, and *Outlook*, 30 December 1893.

2. *Florida Times-Union*, 21 January 1897.

3. Ibid.; Jennings Papers, "Florida Federation of Women's Clubs: Legislation Department" and "A Memorial: Woman's Club of Jacksonville," Box 3, University of Florida Special Collections; Jacksonville Woman's Club, "1897–1898 Program," "Yearbook 1906–1907," Papers, Box 37; *Florida Times-Union*, 23 February 1899.

4. *Florida Times-Union*, 29 April 1900.

5. Ibid., 15 May 1900.

6. Ibid., 15 May 1900, 7 January 1898.

7. Green, *Southern Strategies*, 7–8.

8. Taylor, "The Woman Suffrage Movement," 42–44; National American Woman Suffrage Association, Proceedings of the Forty-Sixth Annual Convention, 12–17 November 1914, 159; Green, *Southern Strategies*, 12–13.

9. Jacksonville Woman's Club, Yearbook, 1903–1904, Yearbook, 1909–1910, Yearbook, 1910–1911, Yearbook, 1913–1914, and Minutes of the Jacksonville Woman's Club, 10 February 1913, 10 March 1913, and 9 February 1914, Papers.

10. National American Woman Suffrage Association, Proceedings, 1914; Wheeler, *New Women*, 112–16.

11. *Florida* Metropolis, 19 and 20 June 1912.

12. Ibid., 17 March 1913.

13. Florida State Federation of Labor, Proceedings of the Convention (1902, 1914, 1917); *Artisan*, 22 May 1915.

14. Today it is Broad and Houston streets.

15. *Florida Metropolis*, 12 February 1915 and 19 June 1915.

16. Ibid., 14 and 17 March 1913; Green, *Southern Strategies*, 28.

17. *Florida Metropolis*, 3 May 1913; National American Woman Suffrage Association, Proceedings, 1914.

18. *Florida Metropolis*, 3 May 1913; National American Woman Suffrage Association, Proceedings, 1914.

19. *Florida Metropolis*, 5 May 1913.

20. Ibid.

21. Ibid., 3, 5, and 9 May 1913.

22. *Florida Metropolis*, 30 May 1913 and 6 November 1913, and *State*, 10 March 1916.

23. *Florida Metropolis*, 12 January 1914, 2 and 3 March 1914, 19 March 1915, and 26 March 1918.

24. May Mann Jennings was the daughter of Austin Jennings, who spoke out against the poll tax during the 1885 Constitutional Convention, and her husband was a cousin of William Jennings Bryan.

25. *Florida Metropolis*, 19 April 1917.

26. Ibid., 19 February 1919.

27. National American Woman Suffrage Association, Proceedings, 1914; *Dixie*, 10 April 1915, and *Florida Metropolis*, 10 May 1917; Green, *Southern Strategies*, 25–29; Wheeler, "Reform, and Reaction," 100–115.

28. Higginbotham, "Clubwomen and Electoral Politics," in *African American Women and the Vote*, edited by Ann D. Gordon et al., eds., 134–55; Terborg-Penn, *African American Women*, 81–106.

29. Eartha M. M. White Collection, Folder Z2, Thomas G. Carpenter Library, University of North Florida; Jacksonville Woman's Club, Minutes of the Jacksonville Woman's Club, 14 February 1916, Papers. On North Carolina, see Gilmore, *Gender and Jim Crow*, 225–28.

30. Ibid.

31. *Florida Metropolis*, 1 June 1903; Eartha M. M. White Collection, Folder Q2, C5.

32. White Collection, Folder O2; *Florida Metropolis*, 12 and 13 February 1913.

33. National Association for the Advancement of Colored People, "Celebration and Annual Meeting 21 November 1917," and McCleary to Johnson, 9 August 1917, NAACP Papers, part 1, Branch Files, G41, Library of Congress; *Florida Metropolis*, 20 November 1917.

34. National Association for the Advancement of Colored People, McCleary to Johnson, 9 and 16 August 1917, NAACP Papers, part 1.

35. National Association for the Advancement of Colored People, McCleary to Johnson, 22 March 1917, and Jacksonville Branch Charter, NAACP Papers, part 1.

36. Ibid., 16 August 1917.

37. Ibid., 22 March 1917.

Conclusion

1. *New York Times*, 10 May 1909.

2. Spear, *Black Chicago*, 223–31; Lakin, "A Dark Night," 1–29; Laurie, "The U.S. Army," 135–43. Race riots were not unique to urban areas during the summer of 1919; see Whayne, "Low Villains and Wickedness," 285–313.

3. National Association for the Advancement of Colored People, Sidney Catts to John Shillady, 18 March 1919, NAACP Papers, part 1, Branch Files, G41, Library of Congress; *Florida Times-Union*, 28 July 1919.

4. *Florida Metropolis*, 21 August 1919.

5. Ibid.

6. *Florida Times-Union*, 22 August 1919 and *Florida Metropolis*, 11 September 1919. Many of the cab drivers were released because they were appearing in a movie. Jacksonville was home to one of the first African American movie studios. During their off hours, hack drivers would act in these films.

7. *Florida Metropolis*, 8 September 1919.

8. *Florida Times-Union*, 9 September 1919; Brundage, *Lynching in the New South*, 84–85.

9. *Florida Times-Union*, 9 September 1919.

10. Ibid.; National Association for the Advancement of Colored People, "Chicago Illinois Journal," 8 September 1919, NAACP Papers, part 1, Branch Files, G41, Library of Congress.

11. *Half Century Magazine*, March 1920 and *Messenger*, March 1920; National Association for the Advancement of Colored People, John Gregg to Mary Ovington, 17 September 1919, NAACP Papers, part 1, Branch Files, G41, Library of Congress.

12. *Florida Times-Union*, 11 and 12 September 1919.

13. Ibid., 10, 12, 17, and 20 September 1919; National Association for the Advancement of Colored People, John Gregg to John Shillady, 10 September 1919, NAACP Papers, part 1, Branch Files, G41, Library of Congress.

14. National Association for the Advancement of Colored People, John Gregg to John Shillady, 10 September 1919, NAACP Papers, part 1, Branch Files, G41, Library of Congress.

15. *Florida Times Union*, 26 and 27 September 1919.

16. *Florida Metropolis*, 27 September 1919.

17. Ibid., 3, 4, 5, and 6 October 1919; *Florida Times-Union*, 9 October 1919; Joel Williamson, *A Rage for Order*, 133–41.

18. *Florida Metropolis*, 17 October 1919.

19. Ibid.

20. *Half Century Magazine*, March 1920, and *Messenger*, March 1920.

21. Florida State Federation of Labor, Proceedings 1920.

22. Ibid.

23. *New York Age*, 1 May 1920.

24. For more information about pink tea parties, consult "A Pink Tea Party," *Ladies Home Journal and Practical Housekeeping* 2 (November 1885): 2; S. O. Johnson, "Hints Upon Etiquette and Good Manners," *Ladies Home Journal and Practical Housekeeping* 3 (July 1886): 11.

25. *Florida Metropolis*, 24 March 1920 and 8 September 1920.

26. Ibid., 16 and 27 September 1920, 7 October 1920; Jennings Papers, S. B. Jennings to May Jennings, 9 September 1920.

27. *Florida Metropolis*, 8, 27, and 28 October 1920; National Association for the Advancement of Colored People, Janice Lowder to NAACP, 11 October 1920, NAACP Papers, part 4 [Microfilm], reel 1.

28. *Florida Metropolis*, 31 October 1920.

29. Ibid.

30. National Association for the Advancement of Colored People, Johnson to Hills, 29 and 31 October 1920, NAACP Papers, part 4.

31. *Florida Times-Union*, 30 October 1920; White, "Election By Terror," 195–97; White, "Election Day," 106; Office of the Florida Secretary of State, Election Returns 1920, Certificate of the County Canvasses," vol. 22.

32. Office of the Florida Secretary of State, Election Returns 1920; White, "Election By Terror," 195. Also see National Association for the Advancement of Colored People, Floyd to Johnson, 2 November 1920; Floyd to White, 7 December 1920; and Johnson to Tinkham, 6 December 1920—all in NAACP Papers, part 4, reel 1.

33. White, "Election By Terror," 195; National Association for the Advancement of Colored People, Alexander Akerman to Senator William C. Kenyon, 2 November 1920, NAACP Papers, part 4, reel 1.

34. Ibid.

35. White, "Election Day," 109.

36. Ibid., "Election By Terror," 195.

Epilogue

1. Johnson, *Along This Way*, 45.

2. Fraser, "Rethinking the Public Sphere," 109–42; Ryan, *Civic Wars*, 183–227.

3. Ellison, *Invisible Man*, 3.

4. Korstad and Lichtenstein, "Opportunities Found and Lost," 786–811; Korstad, *Civil Rights Unionism*, 1–12; Morris, *The Origins of the Civil Rights Movement*, ix; Honey, *Southern Labor*, 1–12; Robin D. G. Kelley, *Hammer and Hoe*, 13–33; Gilmore, *Defying Dixie*, 15–66.

5. Gilmore, *Defying Dixie*, 1–14; Blair L. M. Kelley, *Right to Ride*, 15–32.

Bibliography

PRIMARY SOURCES

ARCHIVES

American Missionary Association Archives. Manuscript, 1983 microfilm edition. Amistad Research Center, New Orleans.

Baldwin, George Johnson. Papers, 1884–1936. Southern Historical Collection at the Wilson Library, University of North Carolina at Chapel Hill.

Black Workers in the Era of the Great Migration, 1916–1925. Microfilm project of University Publications of America. Edited by James R. Grossman. Frederick, Md.: University Publications of America, 1985.

Bureau of Refugees, Freedmen, and Abandoned Lands. Records of the Assistant Commissioner and Subordinate Field Offices for the State of Florida, 1865–1872. Microfilm. Record Group M1869, National Archives and Records Administration (NARA) at Atlanta.

Cookman Institute of Jacksonville, Florida. *Catalogue of Cookman Institute, 1886–1887.* Central Florida Memory Project. Accessed 2 September 2011. http://www.cfmemory. org/.

Eartha M. M. White Collection. Special Collections, University of North Florida.

Florida State Federation of Labor. Proceedings of the Convention (1902, 1914, and 1917). George A. Smathers Libraries Special Collections, University of Florida.

Jacksonville Woman's Club. Papers. Jacksonville Historical Society, Jacksonville, Fla.

Jennings, May Mann. Papers, 1889–1963. George A. Smathers Libraries Special Collections, University of Florida.

L'Engle, Edward M. Papers, 1834–1907. Southern Historical Collection at the Wilson Library, University of North Carolina at Chapel Hill.

National American Woman Suffrage Association. *Proceedings of the National American Woman Suffrage Association Forty-Sixth Annual Convention, 1914.* New York: National American Woman Suffrage Association, 1914.

National Association for the Advancement of Colored People. Papers of the NAACP. Part 1: 1909–1950. NAACP Branch Files. Manuscript Division, Library of Congress.

———. Papers of the NAACP. Part 4: The Voting Rights Campaign, 1916–1950. Microfilm project of University Publications of America. Frederick, Md.: University Publications of America, 1986.

Union Republican Club of Jacksonville. Proceedings, 27 March 1867–25 July 1867. Misc. Manuscripts Collection 8, Florida Historical Society, Cocoa, Fla.

United Brotherhood of Carpenters and Joiners of America. "List of Local Unions." *Official Handbook.* 1892.

LEGAL PROCEEDINGS

Civil Rights Cases, 109 U.S. 3 (1883).

Crooms *v.* Schad, 51 Fla. 168, 40 So. 497 (1906).

Florida *v.* Andrew Patterson, Florida Reports 50 (1905).

Florida East Coast Railroad Company *v.* Geiger, 64 Fla., 60 So. 753 (1914).

Florida Supreme Court. Purcell v. State: Introductory Statement of Nature and Result of Suit. June Term 1905. State of Florida Archives, Tallahassee.

———. Purcell v. State: Introductory Statement and Result of Suit; Opinion: Judgment Affirmed. June Term 1905. State of Florida Archives, Tallahassee.

Patterson *v.* Taylor, 51 Fla. 275, 40 So. 493 (1906).

Smith *v.* Burbridge, 24 Fla. 112, 3 So. 869 (1888).

Williams *v.* Jacksonville, Tampa, and Key West Railroad, 26 Fla. 533, 8 So. 446 (1890).

GOVERNMENT DOCUMENTS

Florida

City of Jacksonville. *Charter and Ordinances of the City of Jacksonville: Together with the Rules and Important Resolutions of the City Council.* 1889. Jacksonville, Fla.: Chas. W. DaCosta, 1889.

———. *Charter and Ordinances of the City of Jacksonville: Together with the Rules and Important Resolutions of the City Council.* 1901. Jacksonville, Fla.: Chas. W. DaCosta and F. W. Dennis and Sons, 1901. Florida Heritage Collection, Jacksonville Historical Society.

———. *Charter and Ordinances for the City of Jacksonville.* 1917. Compiled and produced in Jacksonville, Fla. Florida Heritage Collection, Jacksonville Historical Society.

————. Jacksonville City Council Minutes, 1901–1920. Records Office.

————. *Jacksonville City Directory, 1870–1920*. Jacksonville Public Library.

————. *Ordinances of the City of Jacksonville*. Jacksonville, Fla.: C. Drew's Book and Job Printing Office, 1868. Jacksonville Public Library.

Florida Department of Education. "Biennial Report of the Superintendent of Instruction, 1890–1897." University of Florida, Special Collections.

Florida House of Representatives. Annual Report of the Treasurer of the State of Florida. *Journal of the House of Representatives 1895*. Tallahassee: John G. Collins State Printer, 1895.

————. *Journal of the House of Representatives 1905*. State of Florida Archives, Tallahassee.

Florida State Senate. *Journal of the Senate 1905*. State of Florida Archives, Tallahassee.

Office of the Florida Secretary of State. Election Returns 1920, Certificate of the County Canvasses. Vol. 22. State of Florida Archives, Tallahassee.

City of Pensacola. City Council Minutes. 1905.

Railroad Commission of the State of Florida. "Annual Report of the Seaboard Air Line Railway Company." 31 December 1916. State of Florida Archives, Tallahassee.

State of Florida. *Acts and Resolutions*. 1866–1915. Library of the Supreme Court of Florida.

————. Constitution. 1865, 1868, 1885. State of Florida Archives.

————. *Digest of the School Laws of the State of Florida*. Tallahassee: T. J. Appleyard, 1915.

————. *Journal of the Proceedings of the Constitutional Convention*. Tallahassee: N. M. Bowen State Printer, 1885.

————. *Laws of Florida 1887*. State of Florida Archives, Tallahassee.

United States

General Court-Martial Records, United States Colored Troops (U.S.C.T.). Record Group 153, National Archives and Records Administration.

Records of the United States Army Continental Commands, 1821–1920. Record Group 393, National Archives and Records Administration.

U.S. Bureau of the Census. Fourteenth Census of the United States. Vol. 2: Population 1920, General Report and Analytical Tables. Washington, D.C.: U.S. Government Printing Office, 1922.

————. Fourteenth Census of the United States, Taken in the Year 1920. Vol. 6, part 2: Agriculture, Reports by States, with Statistics for Counties Alabama–Montana. Washington D.C.: U.S. Government Printing Office, 1922.

————. Fourteenth Census of the United States, Taken in the Year 1920. Vol. 8: Manufactures 1919, General Reports and Analytical Tables. Washington D.C.: U.S. Government Printing Office, 1923.

————. Fourteenth Census of the United States, Taken in the Year 1920. Vol. 9: Manufactures 1919, Reports for the States, with Statistics for Principal Cities. Washington D.C.: U.S. Government Printing Office, 1923.

————. Thirteenth Census of the United States, Taken in the Year 1910. Vol. 1: Population

1910, General Reports and Analysis. Washington, D.C.: U.S. Government Printing Office, 1913.

———. Thirteenth Census of the United States, Taken in the Year 1910. Vol. 6: Agriculture 1909 and 1910, Reports by States, with Statistics for Counties Alabama–Montana. Washington D.C.: U.S. Government Printing Office, 1913.

———. Thirteenth Census of the United States, Taken in the Year 1910. Vol. 6: Manufactures 1909, General Report and Analysis. Washington D.C.: U.S. Government Printing Office, 1913.

———. United States Census of Agriculture 1925: Reports for States with Statistics for Counties. Part 2. Washington D.C.: U.S. Government Printing Office, 1927.

NEWSPAPERS

Afro American Ledger (Baltimore), 1905.
American Missionary (New York), 1888–1901.
Artisan (Jacksonville), 1914–1919.
Atlanta Constitution, 1901.
Carpenter (Seat Pleasant, Md.), 1902.
Christian Advocate (New York), 1866–1890.
Christian Index (Atlanta), 1892–1896.
Christian Recorder (Philadelphia), 1864–1888.
Christian Standard (Cincinnati), 1870–1890.
Cleveland Gazette, 1905.
Colored American (Washington, D.C.), 1905.
Congregationalist (Boston), 1870–1888.
Daily Florida Standard (Jacksonville), 1891–1892.
Dixie (Jacksonville), 1912.
Evening Telegram (Jacksonville), 1893.
Fernandina Florida Mirror, 1880.
Florida Metropolis (Jacksonville), 1901–1920.
Florida Times (Jacksonville), 1866–1868.
Florida Times-Union (Jacksonville), 1885–1920.
Florida Union (Jacksonville), 1865–1877.
Freeman (Indianapolis), 1905.
Half Century Magazine (New York), 1920.
Herald (Jacksonville), 1866–1869.
Huntsville Gazette (Alabama), 1882.
Independent (New York), 1892–1896, 1913.
Liberator (Boston), 1865.
Mercury and Floridian (Jacksonville), 1869.
Messenger (New York), 1920.
Newark Daily Advertiser, 1869.
New York Age, 1888–1905.
New York Evangelist, 1884.

New York Freeman, 1885–1887.
New York Globe, 1883–1884.
New York Observer and Chronicle, 1874.
New York Times, 1865–1909.
Outlook (New York), 1915.
North American (Philadelphia), 1892.
Pensacola Journal, 1905.
Savannah Labor Herald, 1912.
Savannah Morning News, 1870–1885.
Savannah Tribune, 1912.
St. Augustine Examiner, 1869.
State (Jacksonville), 1916.
Tallahassee Sentinel, 1868–1870.
Tallahassee Weekly Floridian, 1869–1873.
Washington Bee (Washington, D.C.), 1905.
Weekly Pelican (New Orleans), 1882.
Western Christian Advocate (Cincinnati), 1883.
Wichita Search (Wichita), 1905.
Zion's Herald and Wesleyan Journal (Boston), 1864–1888.

SECONDARY SOURCES

Akin, Edward N. "When a Minority Becomes the Majority: Blacks in Jacksonville Politics 1887–1907." *Florida Historical Quarterly* 53 (October 1974): 123–45.

Arnesen, Eric. *Brotherhoods of Color: Black Railroad Workers and the Struggle for Equality*. Cambridge: Harvard University Press, 2001.

———. "Like Banquo's Ghost, It Will Not Down": The Race Question and the American Railroad Brotherhoods, 1880–1920." *American Historical Review* 99 (December 1994): 1601–633.

Asen, Robert, and Daniel C. Brouwer, eds. *Counterpublics and the State*. Albany: State University of New York Press, 2001.

Ayers, Edward L. *The Promise of the New South: Life after Reconstruction*. New York: Oxford University Press, 1992.

Bakhtin, Mikhail. *Rabelais and His World*. Translated by Hélène Iswolsky. Bloomington: Indiana University Press, 2008.

Beck, E. M., and Stewart E. Tolnay. "The Killing Fields of the Deep South: The Market for Cotton and the Lynching of Blacks, 1882–1930." *American Sociological Review* 55 (August 1990): 526–39.

Bender, Thomas, ed. *Rethinking American History in a Global Age*. Berkeley: University of California Press, 2002.

Bennett, B. Kevin. "The Jacksonville Mutiny." *Civil War History* 38 (March 1992): 39–50.

Boris, Eileen. "From Gender to Racialized Gender: Laboring Bodies That Matter." *International Labor and Working-Class History* 63 (Spring 2003): 9–13.

Brundage, Fitzhugh W. *Lynching in the New South: Georgia and Virginia, 1880–1930.* Urbana: University of Illinois Press, 1993.

Camp, Stephanie M. H. "'I Could Not Stay There': Enslaved Women, Truancy, and the Geography of Everyday Forms of Resistance in the Antebellum Plantation South." *Slavery and Abolition* 23 (December 2002): 1–20.

———. *Closer to Freedom: Enslaved Women and Everyday Resistance in the Plantation South.* Chapel Hill: University of North Carolina Press, 2004.

Campbell, Walter E. "Profits, Prejudice, and Protest: Utility Competition and the Generation of Jim Crow Streetcars in Savannah, 1905–1907." *Georgia Historical Quarterly* 70 (Summer 1986): 197–200.

Chalmers, David. "The Ku Klux Klan in the Sunshine State: The 1920s." *Florida Historical Quarterly* 42 (January 1964): 209–13.

"The Co-Operative Movement." *American Socialist* 4 (24 April 1879): 131.

Cox, Merlin G. "Military Reconstruction in Florida." *Florida Historical Quarterly* 46 (January 1968): 219–33.

Crawford, Margret. "Contesting the Public Realm: Struggles over Public Spaces in Los Angeles." *Journal of Architectural Education* 49 (September 1995): 4–9.

Cresswell, Tim. *In Place/Out of Place: Geography, Ideology, and Transgression.* Minneapolis: University of Minnesota Press, 1996.

Crewdson, Arlene Joan. "Invisibility: A Study of the Works of Toomer, Wright, and Ellison." Ph.D. diss. Loyola University Chicago, 1974.

Crooks, James B. "The Changing Face of Jacksonville, Florida 1900–1910." *Florida Historical Quarterly* 62 (April 1984): 441–63.

———. *Jacksonville after the Fire, 1901–1919: A New South City.* Gainesville: University Press of Florida, 1991.

———. "Jacksonville in the Progressive Era: Responses to Urban Growth." *Florida Historical Quarterly* 65 (July 1986): 52–71.

Davis, Frederick T. *History of Jacksonville, Florida, and Vicinity, 1513 to 1924.* Gainesville: University of Florida Press, 1964.

Davis, Lennard J. "The Social Construction of Public Locations." *Browning Institute Studies* 17 (1989): 23–40.

Davis, Mike. "Fortress Los Angeles: The Militarization of Urban Space." In *Variations on a Theme Park: The New American City and the End of Public Space.* Edited by Michael Sorkin, 154–80. New York: Farrar, Straus, and Giroux, 1992.

Dawson, Michael C. *Black Visions: The Roots of Contemporary African-American Political Ideologies.* Chicago: University of Chicago Press, 2001.

Douglass, Frederick. "The Color Line." *North American Review* 132 (June 1881): 567–77.

Du Bois, W.E.B. *Black Reconstruction.* New York: Harcourt, Brace, 1935. Reprint, New York: Atheneum, 1992.

———. *The Souls of Black Folk.* New York: A. C. McClurg and Company, 1903. Reprint, New York: Penguin, 1996.

Edwards, P. K. *Strikes in the United States 1881–1974.* New York: St. Martin's Press, 1981.

Ellison, Ralph. *Invisible Man.* 2nd ed. New York: Random House, 1947. Reprint, New York: Vintage 1980.

Fairlie, Margaret C. "The Yellow Fever Epidemic of 1888 in Jacksonville." *Florida Historical Quarterly* 19 (October 1940): 95–108.

Fannin, John F. "The Jacksonville Mutiny of 1865." *Florida Historical Quarterly* 88 (Winter 2010): 388–94.

Foner, Eric. *Reconstruction: America's Unfinished Revolution, 1863–1977.* New York: Harper and Row, 1988.

Foster, John T., and Sarah Whitmer Foster. "The Last Shall Be First: Northern Methodists in Reconstruction Jacksonville." *Florida Historical Quarterly* 70, no. 3 (January 1992): 265–80.

Foster, John T., Jr., Herbert B. Whitmer, Jr., and Sarah W. Foster. "Tourism Was Not the Only Purpose: Jacksonville Republicans and Newark's Sentinel of Freedom." *Florida Historical Quarterly* 63 (January 1985): 318–24.

Frank, Dana. "White Working Class Women and the Race Question." *International Labor and Working Class History* 54 (1998): 80–102.

Fraser, Nancy. "Rethinking the Public Sphere: A Contribution to the Critique of Actually Existing Democracy." In *Habermas and the Public Sphere.* Edited by Craig Calhoun, 109–42. Cambridge, Mass.: MIT Press, 1992.

Gaines, Kevin K. *Uplifting the Race: Black Leadership, Politics, and Culture in the Twentieth Century.* Chapel Hill: University of North Carolina Press, 1996.

Gilmore, Elizabeth. *Defying Dixie: The Radical Roots of Civil Rights, 1919–1950.* New York: W. W. Norton, 2008.

———. *Gender and Jim Crow: Women and the Politics of White Supremacy in North Carolina, 1896–1920.* Chapel Hill: University of North Carolina Press, 1996.

Goings, Kenneth W., and Raymond A. Mohl. "Toward a New African American Urban History." In *The New African American Urban History.* Edited by Kenneth W. Goings and Raymond A. Mohl, 1–13. Thousand Oaks, Calif.: Sage, 1996.

Goodwin, Gary V. "Joseph E. Lee of Jacksonville, 1880–1920: African American Political Leadership in Florida." M.A. thesis, Florida State University, 1996.

Gordon, Ann D., Bettye Collier-Thomas, John H. Bracey, Alrene Voski Avakian, and Joyce Avrech Berkman, eds. *African American Women and the Vote 1837–1965.* Amherst: University of Massachusetts Press, 1997.

Gordon, Fon Louise. *Caste and Class: The Black Experience in Arkansas, 1880–1920.* Athens: University of Georgia Press, 1995.

Green, Elna C. *Southern Strategies: Southern Women and the Woman Suffrage Question.* Chapel Hill: University of North Carolina Press, 1997.

Habermas, Jürgen. *Strukturwandel der Öffentlichkeit.* Federal Republic of Germany: Hermann Luchterhand Verlag, 1962. Translated by Thomas Burger and Frederick Lawrence as *The Structural Transformation of the Public Sphere: An Inquiry into a Category of Bourgeois Society.* Cambridge, Mass.: MIT Press, 1991.

Hale, Grace Elizabeth. *Making Whiteness: The Culture of Segregation in the South, 1890–1940.* New York: Pantheon Books, 1998.

Hardwick, Kevin R. "Your Old Father Abe Lincoln is Dead and Damned: Black Soldiers and the Memphis Race Riot of 1866." *Journal of Social History* 27 (Fall 1993): 111–23.

Harvey, David. *Justice, Nature, and the Geography of Difference*. Malden, Mass.: Blackwell Publishing, 1996.

Haulman, C. A. "Changes in the Economic Power Structure in Duval County, Florida, During the Civil War and Reconstruction." *Florida Historical Quarterly* 52, no. 2 (October 1973): 175–84.

Herod, Andrew. *Labor Geographies: Workers and Landscapes of Capitalism*. New York: Guilford Press, 2001.

Higginbotham, Evelyn Brooks. *Righteous Discontent: The Women's Movement in the Black Baptist Church, 1880–1920*. Cambridge, Mass.: Harvard University Press, 1993.

Holston, James. *Insurgent Citizenship: Disjunctions of Democracy and Modernity in Brazil*. Princeton, N.J.: Princeton University Press, 2009.

Honey, Michael K. *Southern Labor and Black Civil Rights: Organizing Memphis Workers*. Urbana: University of Illinois Press, 1993.

Humphreys, Margret. *Yellow Fever and the South*. Brunswick, N.J.: Rutgers University Press, 1994.

Hunter, Tera W. *To 'Joy My Freedom: Southern Black Women's Lives and Labors after the Civil War*. Cambridge, Mass.: Harvard University Press, 1997.

Ingalls, Robert P. *Tampa Urban Vigilantes in the New South, 1882–1936*. Gainesville: University Press of Florida, 1993.

Jackson, Kenneth T. *The Ku Klux Klan in the City, 1915–1930*. New York: Oxford University Press, 1967.

Jepson, Wendy. "Spaces of Labor Activism, Mexican-American Women and the Farm Worker Movement in South Texas since 1996." *Antipode* 37 (September 2005): 679–702.

Johnson, James Weldon. *Along This Way: The Autobiography of James Weldon Johnson*. New York: Viking Press, 1933. Reprint Boston: De Capo Press 2000.

Jones, Jacqueline. *Labor of Love Labor of Sorrow: Black Women, Work, and the Family from Slavery to the Present*. New York: Basic Books, 1985.

Keller, Lisa. *Triumph of Order: Democracy and Public Space in New York and London*. New York: Columbia University Press, 2008.

Kelley, Blair L. M. *Right to Ride: Streetcar Boycotts and African American Citizenship in the Era of Plessy v. Ferguson*. Chapel Hill: University of North Carolina Press, 2010.

Kelley, Robin D. G. *Hammer and Hoe: Alabama Communists During the Great Depression*. Chapel Hill: University of North Carolina Press, 1990.

———. *Race Rebels: Culture, Politics, and the Black Working Class*. New York: Free Press, 1994.

———. "'We Are Not What We Seem': Rethinking Black Working-Class Opposition in the Jim Crow South." *Journal of American History* 80 (June 1993): 75–112.

Kharif, Wali R. "Black Reaction to Segregation and Discrimination in Post-Reconstruction Florida." *Florida Historical Quarterly* 64 (October 1985): 162–63.

Korstad, Robert. *Civil Rights Unionism: Tobacco Workers and the Struggle for Democracy in the Mid-Twentieth-Century South*. Chapel Hill: University of North Carolina Press, 2003.

Korstad, Robert, and Nelson Lichtenstein. "Opportunities Found and Lost: Labor, Radicals, and the Early Civil Rights Movement." *Journal of American History* 75 (December 1988): 786–811.

Kousser, J. Morgan. *The Shaping of Southern Politics Suffrage Restriction and the Establishment of the One-Party South, 1880–1910.* New Haven, Conn.: Yale University Press, 1974.

Lakin, Matthew. "'A Dark Night': The Knoxville Race Riot of 1919." *Journal of East Tennessee History* 72 (2000): 1–29.

Landes, Joan B. *Women and the Public Sphere in the Age of the French Revolution.* Ithaca, N.Y.: Cornell University Press, 1988.

Lassiter, Matthew D., and Joseph Crespino. "Introduction: The End of Southern History." In *The Myth of Southern Exceptionalism.* Edited by Matthew D. Lassiter and Joseph Crespino, 3–22. New York: Oxford University Press, 2010.

Laurie, Clayton D. "The U.S. Army and the Omaha Race Riot of 1919." *Nebraska History* 72 (Spring 1991): 135–43.

Lefebvre, Henri. *Production de l'espace.* Paris: Éditions Anthropos, 1974. Translated by Donald Nicholoson-Smith as *The Production of Space.* Malden, Mass.: Blackwell Publishing, 1991.

Letwin, Daniel. *The Challenge of Interracial Unionism: Alabama Coal Miners, 1878–1921.* Chapel Hill: University of North Carolina Press, 1998.

Litwack, Leon F. *Been in the Storm So Long: The Aftermath of Slavery.* New York: Vintage Books, 1980.

———. *North of Slavery: The Negro in the Free States, 1790–1860.* Chicago: University of Chicago Press, 1961.

———. *Trouble in the Mind: Black Southerners in the Age of Jim Crow.* New York: Alfred A. Knopf, 1999.

Lopes de Souza, Marcelo. "Cities for People, Not for Profit—From a Radical Libertarian and Latin American Perspective." *City* 13 (December 2009): 483–92.

MacLean, Nancy. *Behind the Mask of Chivalry: The Making of the Second Ku Klux Klan.* New York: Oxford University Press, 1994.

Mayer, Margit. "'The Right to the City' in the Context of Shifting Mottos of Urban Social Movements." *City* 13 (June–September 2009): 362–74.

McKiven, Henry M., Jr. *Iron and Steel: Class, Race, and Community in Birmingham, Alabama, 1875–1920.* Chapel Hill: University of North Carolina Press, 1995.

Meier, August, and Elliott Rudwick. *Along the Color Line: Explorations in the Black Experience.* Urbana: University of Illinois Press, 1976.

———. "The Boycott Movement Against Jim Crow Streetcars in the South, 1900–1906." *Journal of American History* 55 (March 1969): 745–75.

Moore, Leonard J. "Historical Interpretations of the 1920's Klan: The Traditional View and the Populist Revision." *Journal of Social History* 24 (Winter 1990): 341–57.

Morris, Aldon D. *The Origins of the Civil Rights Movement: Black Communities Organizing for Change.* New York: Free Press, 1984.

Mumford, Kevin J. "'Lost Manhood' Found: Male Sexual Impotence and Victorian Culture in the United States." *Journal of the History of Sexuality* 3, no. 1 (1992): 33–57.

Norwood, Stephen H. *Strikebreaking and Intimidation: Mercenaries and Masculinity in Twentieth-Century America*. Chapel Hill: University of North Carolina Press, 2002.

Ortiz, Paul. *Emancipation Betrayed: The Hidden History of Black Organizing and White Violence in Florida from Reconstruction to the Bloody Election of 1920*. Berkeley: University of California Press, 2005.

Payne, Daniel Alexander. *Recollections of Seventy Years*. New York: Arno Press, 1968.

Peek, Ralph L. "Aftermath of Military Reconstruction, 1868–1869," *Florida Historical Quarterly* 43, no. 2 (1965): 123–41.

——. "Curbing of Voter Intimidation in Florida, 1871," *Florida Historical Quarterly* 44, no. 3 (1966): 333–48.

——. "Military Reconstruction and the Growth of Anti-Negro Sentiment in Florida, 1867." *Florida Historical Quarterly* 47, no. 4 (1967): 380–400.

Perman, Michael. *The Road to Redemption: Southern Politics, 1869–1879*. Chapel Hill: University of North Carolina Press, 1984.

——. *Struggle for Mastery: Disfranchisement in the South, 1888–1908*. Chapel Hill: University of North Carolina Press, 2001.

Rabinowitz, Howard N. "The Conflict Between Blacks and the Police in the Urban South, 1865–1900." *Historian* 9 (November 1976): 52–79.

——. "More than the Woodward Thesis: Assessing the Strange Career of Jim Crow." *Journal of American History* 75 (December 1988): 842–56.

——. *Race Relations in the Urban South, 1865–1890*. New York: Oxford University Press, 1978.

Richardson, Barbara Ann. "A History of Blacks in Jacksonville, Florida, 1860–1895: A Socioeconomic and Political Study." Ph.D. diss., Carnegie-Mellon University, 1975.

Richardson, Joe M. "Florida Black Codes." *Florida Historical Quarterly* 47, no. 4 (1969): 365–79.

——. *The Negro in the Reconstruction of Florida, 1865–1877*. Tallahassee: Florida State University, 1965.

——. "'The Nest of Vile Fanatics': William N. Sheats and the Orange Park School." *Florida Historical Quarterly* 64 (Spring 1986) 339–406.

——. "'We Are Truly Doing Missionary Work': Letters from American Missionary Association Teachers in Florida, 1864–1874." *Florida Historical Quarterly* 54 (October 1975): 178–95.

Robinson, Charles Frank, II. *Dangerous Liaisons: Sex and Love in the Segregated South*. Fayetteville: University of Arkansas Press, 2003.

Roediger, David R. *The Wages of Whiteness: Race and the Making of the American Working Class*. New York: Verso, 1991.

Russell, Albert J. *Life and Labors of Albert J. Russell*. Jacksonville: DaCosta Printing Company, 1897.

Ryan, Mary P. *Civic Wars: Democracy and Public Life in the American City during the Nineteenth Century*. Berkley: University of California Press, 1997.

——. *Women in Public: Between Banners and Ballots, 1825–1880*. Baltimore, Md.: Johns Hopkins University Press, 1990.

Schwartz, Gerald, ed. *A Woman Doctor's Civil War: Esther Hill Hawks' Diary*. Columbia: University of South Carolina Press, 1984.

Scott, Emmett J. "Additional Letters of Negro Migrants of 1916–1917." *Journal of Negro History* 4 (October 1919): 427–45.

———. "Letters of the Negro Migrants of 1916–1918." *Journal of Negro History* 4 (July 1919): 315–40.

Seidman, Steven. "The Power of Desire and the Danger of Pleasure: Victorian Sexuality Reconsidered." *Journal of Social History* 24, no. 1 (1990): 47–67.

Sewell, Jessica Ellen. *Women and the Everyday City: Public Space in San Francisco, 1890–1915*. Minneapolis: University of Minnesota Press, 2011.

Shofner, Jerrel H. "Florida: A Failure of Moderate Republicanism." In *Reconstruction and Redemption in the South*. Edited by Otto H. Olsen, 13–46. Baton Rouge: Louisiana State University Press, 1980.

———. "Florida and the Black Migration." *Florida Historical Quarterly* 57 (January 1979): 267–88.

———. "The Labor League of Jacksonville: A Negro Union and White Strikebreakers." *Florida Historical Quarterly* 50, (January 1972): 278–82.

———. "Militant Negro Laborers in Reconstruction Florida." *Journal of Southern History* 13 (November 1972): 388–400.

———. "Negro Laborers and the Forest Industries in Reconstruction Florida." *Journal of Forest History* 19 (October 1975): 182–88.

———. *Nor Is It Over Yet: Florida in the Era of Reconstruction, 1863–1877*. Gainesville: University Presses of Florida, 1974.

Spear, Allen H. *Black Chicago: The Making of a Negro Ghetto, 1890–1920*. Chicago: University of Chicago Press, 1967.

Stallybrass, Peter, and Allon White. *The Politics of Poetics of Transgression*. London: Methuen, 1986.

Taylor, A. Elizabeth. "The Woman Suffrage Movement in Florida." *Florida Historical Quarterly* 36 (July 1957): 42–60.

Taylor, Robert A. "Crime and Race Relations in Jacksonville 1884–1892." *Southern Studies* 2 (Spring 1991): 19–33.

Terborg-Penn, Rosalyn. *African American Women in the Struggle for the Vote, 1850–1920*. Bloomington: Indiana University Press, 1998.

Tolnay, Stewart, and E. M. Beck. "Racial Violence and Black Migration in the American South, 1910–1930." *American Sociological Review* 57 (February 1992): 103–16.

Warner, Michael. *Publics and Counterpublics*. New York: Zone Books, 2005.

Webb, Wanton S., ed. *Webb's Historical, Industrial and Biographical Florida, Part 1*. New York: W. S. Webb and Co., 1885.

Welke, Barbara Y. "When All the Women Were White and All the Blacks Were Men: Gender, Class, Race, and the Road to Plessy, 1885–1914." *Law and History Review* 13 (Fall 1995): 261–316.

Whaley, Deborah Elizabeth. *Disciplining Women: Alpha Kappa Alpha, Black Counterpublics, and the Cultural Politics of Black Sororities*. Albany: State University of New York Press, 2010.

Whayne, Jeannie M. "Low Villains and Wickedness in High Places: Race and Class in the Elaine Riots." *Arkansas Historical Quarterly* 58 (Spring 1999): 285–313.

Wheeler, Marjorie Spruill. *New Women of the New South: The Leaders of the Woman Suffrage Movement in the Southern States.* New York: Oxford University Press, 1993.

———. "Reform, and Reaction at the Turn of the Century: Southern Suffragists, the NAWSA, and the 'Southern Strategy' in Context." In *Votes for Women: The Struggle for Suffrage Revisited.* Edited by Jean H. Baker, 102–17. New York: Oxford University Press, 2002.

White, Walter F. "Election by Terror in Florida." *New Republic* 25 (12 January 1921): 195–97.

———. "Election Day in Florida." *Crisis* (January 1921): 106–9.

Wilbanks, William. *Forgotten Heroes: Police Officers Killed in Early Florida, 1840–1925.* New York: Turner Publishing, 1998.

Williamson, Edward C. "Black Belt Political Crisis: The Savage-James Lynching 1882." *Florida Historical Quarterly* 45 (April 1967): 402–9.

———. "The Constitutional Convention of 1885." *Florida Historical Quarterly* 41 (October 1962): 116–26.

———. *Florida Politics in the Gilded Age, 1877–1893.* Gainesville: University Presses of Florida, 1976.

Williamson, Joel. *The Crucible of Race: Black-White Relations in the American South since Emancipation.* New York: Oxford University Press, 1984.

———. *A Rage for Order: Black/White Relations in the American South since Emancipation.* New York: Oxford University Press, 1986.

Woodward, C. Vann. *The Strange Career of Jim Crow.* New York: Oxford University Press, 1955.

"Workingmen's Associations." *Scientific American* 26 (23 June 1866): 430.

Index

Robert Cassanello is associate professor of history at the University of Central Florida. He is coeditor of *Migration and the Transformation of the Southern Workplace since 1945* with Colin J. Davis and of *Florida's Working-Class Past: Current Perspectives on Labor, Race, and Gender from Spanish Florida to the New Immigration* with Melanie Shell-Weiss.

The University Press of Florida is the scholarly publishing agency for the State University System of Florida, comprising Florida A&M University, Florida Atlantic University, Florida Gulf Coast University, Florida International University, Florida State University, New College of Florida, University of Central Florida, University of Florida, University of North Florida, University of South Florida, and University of West Florida.